The Debt Trap in Nigeria:

Towards a Sustainable Debt Strategy

Edited by
NGOZI OKONJO-IWEALA,
CHARLES C. SOLUDO,
MANSUR MUHTAR

Africa World Press, Inc.

P.O. Box 1892
Trenton, NJ 08607

P.O. Box 48
Asmara, ERITREA

Africa World Press, Inc.

P.O. Box 1892
Trenton, NJ 08607

P.O. Box 48
Asmara, ERITREA

Copyright © 2003 Nigerian Debt Management Office,
  Ngozi Okonjo-Iweala, Charles C. Soludo, Mansur Muhtar

First Printing, 2003

All rights reserved. No part of this publication may be reproduced, stored in a retrieval system, or transmitted in any form or by any means electronic, mechanical, photocopying, recording, or otherwise without the prior written permission of the publisher.

The findings, interpretations and conclusions expressed here are those of the authors and do not necessarily reflect the views of the institutions where they work or the governments they may represent.

Book and cover design: Roger Dormann

The debt trap in Nigeria : towards a sustainable debt strategy / edited by Ngozi Okonjo-Iweala, Charles Soludo, and Mansur Muhtar.
    p. cm.
Includes bibliographical references and index.
  ISBN 1-59221-000-7 (hard cover) -- ISBN 1-59221-001-5 (pbk.)
  1. Debts, Public--Nigeria--Congresses. 2. Debt relief--Nigeria--Congresses. I. Okonjo-Iweala, Ngozi. II. Soludo, Charles Chukwuma. III. Muhtar, Mansur.
  HJ8842.5 .D433 2002

                                                2002007778

Contents

Acknowledgements v

Acronyms and Abbreviations viii

1. Introduction 1
   Ngozi Okonjo-Iweala, Charles Soludo and Mansur Muhtar

PART I
Debt, Poverty and Development: The Global, Regional and National Context

2. Debt, Poverty, and Inequality: Toward an Exit Strategy for Nigeria and Africa 23
   Charles Soludo

3. Sustainable Debt and Development Strategy in Africa 75
   Cyril Enweze

4. Debt Relief: What Has Been Achieved? What Needs to be Done? 91
   Callisto Madavo

5. External Debt, Capital Flight, and Growth in Nigeria...105
   Ibi S. Ajayi

PART II
Institutional and Governance Issues

6. Sound Practices in Government Debt Management 155
   Graeme Wheeler

7. Managing Nigeria's Debt: Institutional and Governance Aspects 167
   Ngozi Okonjo-Iweala

8. Toward Nigeria's Sustainable Debt Strategy 195
   Mike Obadan

PART III
Exiting the Debt Trap

9. Why Nigeria Needs Debt Cancellation Now....217
   Jeffrey Sachs

10. International Experience of Aid and Debt Strategies: Implications for Nigeria..................225
    Paul Collier

11. A Practical Strategy to Reduce Nigeria's Debt 237
    Matthew Martin

12. A Global Agenda for Dealing With Debt 255
    Ann Pettifor

Acknowledgements

The papers in this book form part of the contributions to the International Conference On Sustainable Debt Strategy for Nigeria held in Abuja in May 2001, and organized by the Debt Management Office (DMO) in collaboration with the African Institute for Applied Economics, Enugu. It therefore, owes much to all those who contributed to the success of the conference.

President Olusegun Obasanjo and Vice President Atiku Abubakar who had identified the debt problem as a priority for Nigeria's new democratic government, enthusiastically endorsed the conference and provided the crucial political support. Credit to the government extends to the various officials who translated government commitment into action at the various stages of the project: The Honorable Minister of Finance, Mallam Adamu Ciroma; the Honorable Minister of State for Finance, Senator Jubril Martins Kuye; and the Secretary to the Federal Government, Chief Ufot Ekaette; the Governor of the Central Bank, Chief Joseph Sanusi, and the Chief of Staff to the President, General Aliyu Mohammed. (Rtd.)

The Director General of the DMO, Akin Arikawe provided overall leadership that ensured the success of the Conference. The Office of the President, and notably the Principal Secretary to the President, Steve Orosanye and the President's Special Assistant for Budget, Oby Ezekwesili, provided invaluable counsel and support. Thanks are also due to Nasir El-Rufai, Director General, Bureau for Public Enterprises (BPE) and to Onyema Ugochukwu, Executive Director of the Niger Delta

Development Commission (NDDC) for their insights and support.

The United Kingdom's Department for International Development (DFID) graciously financed the conference while Crown Agents, United Kingdom, ensured efficient logistical and other support. Our thanks go also to the various DFID officials, Theo Thomas and Paul Spray who worked as part of the Conference Steering Committee to ensure a successful outcome.

We would like to thank all Conference participants including members of the Senate Committee on Local and Foreign Loans, the House Committee on Debt, Loans and Foreign Aid, numerous Nigerian academics, members of Civil Society organizations and international NGOs, representatives of labor organizations, including the student unions, the Nigerian Labor Congress, and the Academic Staff Union of Nigerian Universities, the private sector, all of whom enriched the conference discussions.

Special thanks are also due to members of the diplomatic corps and the international donor community in Abuja, including the British High Commissioner to Nigeria, His Excellency, Mr. Phillips, bilateral agencies including USAID, the international institutions including United Nations Development Program (UNDP), the World Bank, the IMF, the AfDB and the Commonwealth Secretariat for their interest and active participation.

There were many interesting papers presented at the Conference. The papers in this volume represent a select few. We would like to thank our authors for their insights, candor, and above all their contributions to the important national and international debate on the debt issue.

Finally, we wish to acknowledge the invaluable assistance and logistical support of the following: Mohamed Yusuf, Josephine Onwuemene, Alice Storch, Vicky Duncan and Fausat Ahmed. Special thanks are due Chii Akporji for diligent editorial support.

The Editors

Acronyms and Abbreviations

AfDB	African Development Bank
AGOA	Africa Growth Opportunities Act (US)
AIAE	African Institute for Applied Economics
CBN	Central Bank of Nigeria
CDF	Comprehensive Development Framework
CPI	Consumer Price Index
DAC	OECD's Development Assistance Committee
DFID	Department for International Development (UK) Development
DMO	Debt Management Office
DRMS	Debt Recording and Management System
ECA	Economic Commission for Africa
ECOWAS	Economic Community of West African States
ESAF	Enhanced Structural Adjustment Facility
EU	European Union
GDP	Gross Domestic Product
GNP	Gross National Product
HIPC	Highly Indebted Poor Countries Initiative
IBRD	International Bank for Reconstruction and Development
IDA	International Development Association
IDG	International Development Goals
IIRR	Institutional Investor Risk Rating
IMF	International Monetary Fund
IMFC	International Monetary and Finance Committee
MDGS	Millennium Development Goals
NPV	Net Present Value
ODA	Official Development Assistance
OECD	Organization for Economic Cooperation and Development
OPEC	Organization of Petroleum Exporting Countries
PRSPs	Poverty Reduction Strategy Papers
RMCs	Regional Member Countries
SBA	Stand-by Arrangement
SDRs	Special Drawing Rights
SIMA	Statistical Information Management and Analysis Database
WSSD	World Summit on Sustainable Development

1
Introduction

NGOZI OKONJO-IWEALA
CHARLES C. SOLUDO
MANSUR MUHTAR

After decades of dictatorship and misrule, Nigeria, Africa's most populous country and potentially its largest economy, has emerged as a nascent democracy, and its leadership is determined to start anew. However, the average Nigerian is poorer today than in 1972, despite the country's nearly US$300 billion earnings from oil exports between 1973 and 2000. Poverty is deep and pervasive, with about 70 percent of the population in absolute poverty. Infrastructure decay is significant, corruption is endemic, and institutions of governance and accountability are grossly weakened.

The new democratic government, therefore, has a monumental task of re-engineering the society, rebuilding basic infrastructure and institutions, fighting corruption, and, most importantly, restructuring the economy for faster economic growth and poverty reduction. But it faces the historic challenge of having to deliver on these "democracy dividends" in the context of what it has long cited as a huge and largely unsustainable debt burden. External debt is 65 percent of gross domestic product (GDP), while annual debt service is nine times the annual health budget. Domestic debt is also an issue, ballooning to an estimated US$8.6 billion by the end of 2001.

With much of the external borrowing greatly reduced, there is evidence of renewed domestic borrowing by all tiers of government—federal, state, and local governments—as well as government parastatals and resulting in rapid increases in debt including of contingent liabilities. Despite recent moves by the Central Bank of Nigeria and the federal authorities to reestablish control, the situation remains fragile politically and economically in the run up to the 2003 elections. Nigeria is not unique in these experiences. As Enweze, Soludo, and Madavo point out in their papers, several emerging, fragile democracies in Africa and other developing countries face similar daunting challenges.

Much of the public debate on debt and development has mostly been conducted as a shouting match between the donor agencies and the nongovernmental organizations (NGOs) on very broad terms. There is not much literature on an attempt to focus on specific national and regional contexts with a view to promoting a convergence of views on the nature, severity, and implications of the debt burden and debt accumulation process for policy choices. Apart from the issue of sensitization and building public-private sector consensus on the debt issue, there is the fundamental one of crafting a strategy that would leave Nigeria less indebted, and more prosperous, in the medi-

Introduction

um to long term.

As part of the present government's determination to forge a tripartite—public/private sector/international community—consensus on broad issues of policy and the development agenda, the federal government of Nigeria (FGN) organized an international conference to brainstorm the thorny issues of a sustainable debt strategy that is compatible with growth and development. The conference, held in Abuja, Nigeria, on May 17 and 18, 2001, was organized by the Debt Management Office (DMO) in collaboration with the African Institute for Applied Economics (AIAE), Enugu, and with financial support by the U.K. Department for International Development (DFID), while the Crown Agents provided logistical support.

The conference was attended by very senior levels of the executive and legislative branches of government, by President Olusegun Obasanjo, Vice President Atiku Abubakar, Senate President Anyim Pius Anyim, and governors, ministers, special advisers, senators, and members of the House of Representatives. There was also high level participation from the external international finance institutions (IFIs) and the donor community. Private civil organizations, NGOs, academia, the press, labor unions, and student organizations were well represented. The conference was initially planned for 150 participants, but more than 300 people attended, underscoring the importance attached to the debt issue by the participants and by Nigerians at large.

In their opening speeches the Nigerian president and vice president charged the participants to:

- Diagnose the debt problem and identify underlying causes
- Proffer solutions to the compounding of interest and pile up of penalties that multiply the quantum of original borrowings
- Design a debt framework that ensures a functional and early warning signal on a potential debt crisis
- Provide ideas for a debt management framework that would be compatible with meeting the country's huge social needs and aspirations, building on ongoing regional and international experience, and suggest paths for debt sustainability
- Identify the domestic economic conditions that would in the short and medium term make Nigeria's debt burden sustainable
- Identify actions at the international level that would help rid Nigeria of its external debt burden, and provide breathing space for economic and social development.

The conference—Nigeria's first to debate its future in the context of debt overhang—was successful, with 25 presentations and intense discussions and debates, and at the end a consensus was reached about the way forward.

This book is an effort to pull together and share some of the interesting analyses and recommendations that emerged from the conference. The chapters consist of selected essays that focus not only on Nigeria's debt situation but also on the regional and global context for developing country debt, including the merits and demerits of the Heavily Indebted Poor Countries (HIPC) initiative.

While the broad conclusions from the conference papers and discussions are summarized in this introductory chapter, the reader will find the individual chapters rich in insights and on the challenges going forward. Much of the diagnostic is similar, but several papers (Collier, Sachs, Pettifor, Soludo) arrive at interesting but differing recommendations for the Nigerian government and the international community.

Debt in the Context of Nigeria's Development Problems

The onset of the Obasanjo administration has focused attention on the resolution of Nigeria's debt burden, and there has been much lively domestic and international debate about the size of Nigeria's debt. Much of this was due to the initial lack of coherence on Nigeria's side (now resolved) on its debt statistics. A great deal of the discussion in several chapters (Ajayi, Obadan) seeks a balance between a thorough diagnosis of the size, severity and consequences of the debt situation on the one hand and an attempt to situate the debt issue as one of the larger underdevelopment challenges facing Nigeria on the other.

How Much Does Nigeria Owe?

Since 1992, when Nigeria started accumulating payment arrears on her Paris Club debts, the debt figures reported by the country had always differed from those of the IFIs. More recently, with a new DMO in place, and its debt statistics largely reconciled with assistance from DFID and Crown Agents, Nigeria's debt stock as of August 2001 was reported at US$28.4 billion. This figure compares with World Bank and International Monetary Fund (IMF) estimates of US$31.9 billion. (Note that because of differing sources, and the initial uncertainties surrounding Nigeria's debt statistics, the chapters all quote differing figures. However, all figures are within the same $28-$32 billion range for Nigeria's total debt. The figures quoted in this section are the officially sanctioned debt statistics for the country.)

Much of the discrepancy in the figures is accounted for by differences in debt data reporting for Paris Club creditors. World Bank and IMF estimates exceed the estimates of the Nigerian government by more than US$3 billion. The World Bank acknowledges that its estimates of Nigeria's debt are based on an amalgam of creditor data, complemented with World Bank staff analysis and extrapolations, and to a lesser extent on debtor data. In some cases extrapolations are made from reports prepared in the 1990s, since Nigeria has not reported external debt transactions for individual loans to the World Bank since 1992. The IMF has also indicated that its figures are based on reports from Paris Club creditor countries, complemented with IMF staff estimates. In recent reports, both institutions have highlighted the tentativeness of the figures, pending the reconciliation of Nigeria's obligations with the Paris Club.

The Nigerian Government made major efforts in the second half of 2000 to rectify the inadequacies in debt data reporting. One of the primary tasks undertaken by the DMO since its establishment in September 2000 has been to ascertain the actual level of Nigeria's indebtedness. The DMO has been engaged in a process of reconciling the official debt numbers with those of the Paris Club creditors. This process has involved the building up of a comprehensive, computerized inventory of debts, verification of individual loan accounts with creditor statements, and reconciliation meetings with 12 out of the 14 creditor countries, which account for more than 95 percent of the country's Paris Club debts. The reconciliation exercise, which has now been virtually completed, has helped obtain a more accurate reading of Nigeria's external debt obligations.

The DMO reports that as of August 31, 2001, Nigeria's debt stock, excluding penalty interests, amounted to US$28.42 billion. This was made up of obligations to Paris Club creditors at US$22.04 billion, non-Paris Club bilateral creditors at US$111.6 million, multilateral creditors at US$2.89 billion, and commercial creditors at US$3.37 billion. From the reconciliation exercise, the discrepancies recorded between government figures and those of the Paris Club creditors stemmed from the following:

- Inclusion by creditors of previously rejected, short-term private sector claims submitted during the refinancing exercise of the 1980s
- Inclusion by creditors of new claims, including short-term trade arrears, medium and long term as well as post cutoff long-term loans, which were not submitted for rescheduling in the past
- Adoption of different methods of interest rate calculation and varied exchange rates by some creditors

• Creditor practice of applying debt service payments to late/penalty interests in lieu of initially offsetting principal payments due, as expected by the debtor.

During the course of the reconciliation exercise, the previously rejected claims as well as fresh claims from the creditors were subjected to thorough verification. Most of the claims have been rejected, and others are being checked with primary obligors. Proof of ineligibility of these claims has been forwarded to the creditors.

Consequences of the Debt Overhang

In the last decade, the Nigerian debt burden has been increasing at an unsustainable rate. As was indicated, the reconciled external debt of Nigeria as at August 2001 was US$28.42 billion. Contractual debt service obligations (that is, amortization and interest payments due on this debt) exceed US$3 billion per annum. However, actual annual debt service payments for the period 1998–2000 averaged about US$1.5 billion. Even this lower actual payment, the result of rescheduling, is about 20–30 percent of total exports, which in Nigeria's undiversified economy is mainly oil. It is also four times the national education budget, and nine times the public health budget.

Looking forward, projected debt service, after rescheduling and without any new commitments, averages more than US$2 billion per annum (2001–02) or a total of about US$43 billion for the rescheduling period. This is in comparison with the original US$13 billion borrowed from the Paris Club largely in 1980s, of which US$17 billion has already been paid.

Nigeria's debt overhang is considered severe in the context of its development challenges. Technically, as Martins and Sachs, note, Nigeria as one of the world's 20 poorest countries with a US$300 income per capita should qualify as a Highly Indebted Poor Country (HIPC), and was considered as one until decisions were made to remove it from the list. Nigeria presently has some of the worst social indicators among developing countries. Its chances of meeting the Millennium Development Goals (MDGs) agreed to by the international community are very slim. Currently, about 70 percent of Nigeria's 125 million people live in absolute poverty on a dollar a day or less. Estimates are that it will require an annual GDP growth rate in the order of 7–8 percent in order to halve the number of people in poverty by 2015.

This translates into an investment rate of more than 30 percent per annum. Currently, the national savings rate is about 15 percent. In addition, the country faces daunting challenges of rebuilding a nation badly damaged by decades of military misrule, not least of which was an almost institutionalized corruption. With a new and fragile democracy, most public and private institutions in the economic, political, social, and legal spheres are in need of redirection and rebuilding.

At the same time, there is tremendous pressure on the government to deliver some democracy dividends. Growth has been anemic, at an average of 3 percent per annum over the past five years. This has been insufficient to make a dent on poverty. If economic growth does not accelerate and development continues to stall, then it will be difficult to tackle the debt burden or deal with emerging threats in the health arena such as HIV/AIDS and tuberculosis, all of which are rising in incidence and threatening to further derail economic growth.

Broader National Economic Context for the Debt

A broad consensus that emerges from the chapters, and also from the discussions at the conference, is that, although the debt overhang now constitutes a major problem, it is only a part of the legacy of past mismanagement of the economy. As a part and a symptom of the larger economic problems of Nigeria, the broader issues must be tackled as part of restoring the economy and establishing a sustainable debt strategy.

While the present democratically elected administration has taken important steps in addressing serious structural problems through, for example, its brave privatization program, several fundamental economic problems remain that constrain growth and poverty reduction. Some of the most important issues include:

- *Fragile and inadequate economic policy reforms:* The lack of diversification and competitiveness of the economy is identified as a major constraint to both sustainable poverty reduction and a viable debt strategy. Over reliance on a natural resource, oil, with substantial international price volatility, and no real mechanisms developed by the government to hedge against this, has been and continues to be a risky development strategy.

Introduction

Further, without addressing the riskiness and uncertainty inherent in the investment climate and the huge infrastructural weaknesses, it will be difficult to stem capital flight, and prevent future indebtedness. The debt overhang itself is, of course, one of the disincentives to investors. The flight of capital from the country is now more than twice the size of GDP, and efforts should be made to attract it back.

- *Weak legal and institutional framework for public resource management:* Weak institutional/legal and administrative capacity to design and manage public resources is identified as central to the economic mismanagement and to the debt overhang problem itself. The situation is made more difficult in a decentralized revenue-sharing environment where the state and local government structures and framework are even weaker than at the federal level.
- *Inefficient use of public resources and mismanagement:* The Obasanjo administration has made some improvements in public resource management through the newly established "due process" mechanism to vet public agencies' investment proposals, and through the move to a more efficient public procurement process. Nevertheless, Nigeria has serious problems with fiscal discipline, a plague that continues from previous administrations, and is not helped by pressure within the present administration and from the legislature. This has an impact on overall macroeconomic management leading to inflationary

and exchange rate pressures. In the past, fiscal indiscipline was compounded by corruption, inefficiency, and waste with a direct bearing on the debt burden. For example, Okonjo-Iweala and Obadan cite a survey by the Ministry of Finance that showed that about 40 percent of the projects for which external loans were contracted in the 1980s and 1990s were never started, even though the loans were fully drawn, and of the remaining hardly any of them was economically viable to generate returns to service the debt.

- *Low absorptive capacity of the economy:* Given the weak institutional capacity, and inefficient public sector, the absorptive capacity of the economy is itself a major problem. In essence, there is a mismatch between the need to pump in financial resources to tackle the myriad needs of the economy and society, and the institutional and administrative capacities to manage such resources to avoid waste. Private sector and nongovernment channels may provide a partial answer to this problem to supplement governmental channels, and should be more vigorously explored, while the public sector is being streamlined and strengthened. This points to massive capacity building efforts to enable the implementation of essential public sector roles.

The International Context

Some of the chapters blame the asymmetric power relations, as well as the rules governing international finance, for Nigeria's debt problems. The rules of international finance encouraged debt to accumulate through an often reckless willingness to lend by the international private and sometimes public sectors in the very high interest rate environment of the 1970s and 1980s. When corruption and capital flight followed, and stolen wealth was stored in the western countries, and in offshore financial centers, there was not, and still is not, much appetite by western governments to expose and repatriate the wealth.

A broad consensus emerged that responsibility for the debt problem must be fully shared between Nigeria and its creditors. Creditors are as guilty as Nigerian governments in the accumulation and mismanagement of the debt. Therefore, as Jeffrey Sachs outlines in his chapter, creditors need to be an essential and credible part of the solution. It is not enough for the creditors to distance themselves, or to offer conventional solutions predicated on Nigeria's so-called oil wealth. Creditors must be prepared to take bold actions, to endorse radical proposals to wipe out debt in a context where Nigeria gets its domestic economic house in order.

The Way Forward

Several chapters—Collier, Obadan, Ajayi, Wheeler, and Okonjo-Iweala—proffer suggestions on reducing the debt burden, resuming sustainable development, and evolving a sustainable debt management framework. These range from repudiating the debt to negotiating debt cancellation and strengthening economic management. Recommendations on strengthening the institutional framework for debt management are also made. What follows is a skeletal overview of these suggestions, many of which are complementary:

Pursue debt reduction and outright cancellation from the international community, especially the Paris Club: Nigeria should pursue vigorously all the options for debt relief, including outright cancellation. Although some analysts opted for unilateral repudiation of the debt, the dominant view was that Nigeria should go for a negotiated resolution of the debt. Given Nigeria's low income status, the country is, at the minimum, entitled under the international rules to HIPC treatment—67 percent cancellation of its debt service over three years followed by 67 percent cancellation of its debt stock—regardless of its debt ratios, and should receive this as soon as it establishes a minimal track record. Discussion of any lower reductions, for example, 33 percent or 50 percent, would be penalizing the vast majority of Nigerians who live on a dollar a day or less.

Furthermore, the fact that about 75 percent of Nigeria's external debt is owed to the rich industrial countries (Paris Club) was seen as offering hope in the quest for debt cancellation because of precedents already set by the Paris Club for countries with much higher per capita incomes than Nigeria, such as Poland. The argument against debt cancellation, which is that the multilateral agencies cannot afford it, cannot hold, for the rich industrial countries, still savoring post-Cold War peace dividends. The loss of debt service from Nigeria would hardly make an impact on these countries fiscal accounts. Further, the argument that Nigeria is an oil rich country is simply untenable in light of its large and poor population and its enormous social needs. At the best of times, the oil revenue is only $91 per Nigerian per annum.

Pursue domestic economic reforms: Government should vigorously pursue economic policy reforms, not just as an attempt to meet the requirements of donors for debt reduction, but as a fundamental national imperative. Nigerians understand that regardless of what happens to the debt issue, they need to put their house in order by intensifying the implementation of reforms. Such reforms should address issues such as security, the prohibitive and uncertain cost of doing business, transparency and accountability, macroeconomic stability, efficiency, and competition. The reforms should also address the poor state of infrastructure, enforce the rule of law, and minimize the risks and uncertainties associated with the business environment. There was broad consensus that only reforms that ensure sustainable growth and competitiveness of the economy constitute a sustainable exit strategy from debt and poverty. A major goal of the reforms is to target the return of flight capital and to discourage the transfer of domestic savings abroad.

If the government can convince Nigerians to invest at home through the promotion of appropriate investment climate, then it is estimated that the annual inflow of private investment might more than make up for any future financing gaps. Some African countries with deeper economic reforms are able to attract substantial return of flight capital. For example, as a consequence of Uganda's reforms, the return of flight capital has exceeded the total exports in the last few years. Nigeria should explore such sources of investible funds through further privatization and liberalization in order to enlarge the scope for private sector operation.

A key element of the reforms is also the need to strengthen or reform the institutional/legal and administrative framework for public resource management. This is to ensure effective and efficient utilization of present and future public resources, to prevent the waste and inefficiencies of the past. Among other things, this institutional re-engineering would ensure probity in public resource use, due diligence, transparency, and accountability that bites, with sanctions when standards are not met.

Eschew accumulation of domestic debt: Excessive recourse to domestic debt is not the answer to Nigeria's financing problems. If not well managed, it can cause huge problems for the budget and for the entire domestic financial system. So far, the government and Nigerians in general have worried mostly about external debt, but the domestic debt is also mounting.

There is a need for appropriate mechanisms to be put in place to check the ballooning of domestic debt through federal government borrowing from the Central Bank of Nigeria, and especially through growing borrowing and spending of states and local governments. Such domestic borrowing has implications for the ability of the federal government to maintain macroeconomic stability and should be checked.

Limit external borrowing and mobilize untapped domestic resources: Because of the past poor track record of external debt—the diversion and corruption involved and the limited impact—there was substantial support for Nigeria to either place a moratorium on borrowing or to strictly limit the amount. Any borrowing must be from concessional sources only. In this regard, the government would also need to strictly monitor and avoid implicit or explicit contingent liabilities arising from borrowings, guarantees, or liabilities of any public enterprises or other government entities.

The government should also try to tap into several untapped domestic resources and put those to effective use. Corruption money should be more aggressively pursued abroad and, together with privatization receipts, invested in a trust fund whose annual returns could be used for development purposes. The estimated US$2 billion per annum being lost in flared gas should be recovered through appropriate investments. A careful audit of oil company operations should be undertaken to ensure the country is indeed getting appropriate returns. Information on oil company operations and finances should be made more transparent and publicly shared to encourage responsible corporate behavior and more social investments to assist poor people.

Put systems in place to better manage existing debts and guide future obligations: There was a consensus that government should implement an independent audit of past loans and focus on their use and impact. Where there has been malfeasance, those responsible should be made accountable and brought before the Independent Anti-Corruption and Other Related Offenses Commission. This will signal punitive action for future debt mismanagement.

Nigeria should formulate a national debt policy,

together with a debt management strategy, and both based on sound analysis. The debt policy should be validated through consultations with civil society and once ready, supported with enabling legislation passed by the National Assembly. Effective debt management institutions and arrangements are important and should be put in place because they can contribute to building a more responsible image of the Nigerian government as more effectively managing public resources.

There is good international practice in this area and Nigeria should draw from this. The DMO is a step in the right direction. The DMO should be strengthened with appropriate legislation, human and financial resources, and an appropriate incentives framework to carry out its mandate. Political commitment to sound debt management, especially adhering to legal and accountability frameworks, will be necessary to support the DMO. Participation of and accountability to civil society in monitoring the implementation of debt policy and debt management will also be important. This needs to extend to independent national audit offices and structures for consultations on new borrowing and public spending.

Better debt management institutions and arrangements should be accompanied by better coordination among the many government agencies dealing with the fiscal accounts and with monetary policy. This is important to assure coherence and consistency in monetary and fiscal policy, and their impact in overall economic management.

The government must invest in training and capacity building of national skills for debt management. This will reduce reliance on expatriate consultants and technical assistance which may not be sustainable. Attention should be paid to managing contingent liabilities. There are excellent systems and practices in several countries from which Nigeria can learn (for example, Chile, South Africa, New Zealand, Ireland, and India), especially with regard to a decentralized system of government.

Participate proactively to address the defects of the international financial system: Nigerian policymakers should promote reform of international financial systems and urge countries to review and reform domestic legislation that impedes the return of stolen funds from developing countries.

Promote disclosure and transparency in international financial flows and the enactment of international legislation to govern the transfer of corrupt money, along with appropriate penalties for individuals involved, and for governments that retain such monies. Support an international arbitration/adjudication system to settle disputes between donors/creditors and debtor countries.

While the majority of the suggestions and recommendations from authors in this volume and, indeed from conference deliberations, are appropriately directed at the Nigerian government, there emerged a strong sense that culpability for the debt problem is not Nigeria's alone. The international community was, therefore, called upon to more proactively assist Nigeria in exiting the debt trap, and to enable it to focus its resources on promoting economic growth and on providing the enabling environment for its large population to exit from poverty.

Part 1:
Debt, Poverty and Development: The Global, Regional and National Context

2

Debt, Poverty, and Inequality:
Toward an Exit Strategy for Nigeria and Africa

CHARLES CHUKWUMA SOLUDO
Executive Director, African Institute for Applied Economics, Enugu, Nigeria and Professor of Economics, Department of Economics University of Nigeria, Nsukka

Some 300 million Africans, almost half the population, live on barely US$0.65 a day, and this number is growing relentlessly. Moreover, a severe lack of capabilities—education, health, and nutrition—among Africa's poor threatens to make poverty "dynastic," with the descendants of the poor also remaining poor. Africa is the only region where primary enrollment rates were lower in 1995 than in 1980, and the burden of disease is dramatically higher in Africa than elsewhere. Africa is not only poor, it also suffers from vast inequality in incomes, in assets, in control over *public resources, and in access to essential services, as well as pervasive insecurity. These dimensions of poverty and deprivation are worsening in many parts of the region (World Bank 2000d).*

After 50 years of development finance in the twentieth century, with massive aid and rapid debt accumulation, and decades of several special initiatives to cure poverty in Africa, pervasive poverty and widening inequality persist as the fundamental development challenge of the twenty-first century. Development finance was designed as a response to problems of underdevelopment, but aside from the diamond-rich Botswana, hardly any other country has graduated out of the list of developing countries in more than three decades. Instead, many more countries continue to join the club of destitute nations—now totaling 48, out of which 33 are in Africa. Paradoxically, rather than cure poverty, development finance has now cumulated into largely unpayable debt stocks that some analysts believe to constitute the most fundamental constraint to poverty eradication and sustainable development.[1]

A sustainable debt strategy is one which, over a reasonable time horizon, ensures that the country/region escapes from debt and aid dependence as well as the traps of pervasive poverty and inequality. Despite nearly US$300 billion of oil revenues, high domestic and foreign debt, and dozens of specialized programs in the last four decades directed at poverty, Nigeria remains desperately poor. So is Africa. If Nigeria succeeds in just preventing the worsening of poverty—a tall task given current trends—it would still have some 170 million poor people in 2025. What kind of strategy can leave Nigeria and Africa less indebted and less poor in the longer term, say, in 10–20 years time?

Poverty and Inequality: Some Stylized Facts

Globally, poverty and inequality seem to have worsened in the last two decades (UNDP 1999, pp. 2–3). More than 80 countries still have per capita incomes that are lower than a decade or more ago. About 40 countries have sustained average per capita income growth rate of more than 3 percent a year since 1990, and 55 countries, mostly in Sub-Saharan Africa (SSA) and Eastern Europe and the Commonwealth of Independent States (CIS) have had declining per capita incomes. Within countries, inequality has worsened greatly (especially in the CIS countries) and even within the rich countries since 1980, especially Sweden, the United Kingdom, and the United States. Between countries inequality has worsened greatly with the income gap between the fifth of the world's people living in the richest countries and the fifth in the poorest countries rising to the ratio of 74 to 1 in 1997, up from 60 to 1 in 1990, 30 to 1 in 1960, and 11 to 1 in 1913.

By the late 1990s, the fifth of the world's population living in the highest income countries had 86 percent of the world's gross domestic product (GDP), and the bottom fifth just 1 percent; 82 percent of world export markets, the bottom fifth just 1 percent; 68 percent of foreign direct investment, the bottom fifth just 1 percent; and 74 percent of world's telephone lines, the bottom fifth just 1.5 percent. In 1998, the assets of the top three billionaires were more than the combined gross national product (GNP) of all least developed countries with their 600 million people.

Sub Saharan Africa is a special case,[2] the poorest region of the world, with 33 of the 48 least developed countries (LDCs), and with average per capita income in 1999 less than the level in 1969. Despite modest improvements since independence in the 1960s, SSA lags far behind the rest of the world in terms of basic social indicators. Some of the indicators point to a crisis that is almost peculiar to Africa, and include poor education, high child mortality, and endemic diseases—tuberculosis, malaria, and HIV/AIDS—that impose severe costs on Africa.

So far, none of the seven largest economies in Africa is doing well. The 33 LDCs in Africa are in a much worse situation. With an average per capita income of US$243 in 1999 and 60–80 percent of the 375 million people living on less than US$0.65 a day, poverty is widespread, deep, and severe. With a largely agrarian production base, most of the population lives barely at the subsistence level. Every indicator shows that these countries are likely to remain in this state for some time to come. For example, current estimates indicate that at current trends even the performer in the group, Uganda, will still be an LDC in 2020 (Bethelemy et al. 2001).

With a per capita income level of US$300, Nigeria is one of the 20 poorest countries in the world. Although it is not officially classified as one, the country clearly qualifies as an LDC. The fight against poverty has been a central plank of development planning since independence in 1960. So far, about 15 ministries, 14 specialized agencies, and 19 donor agencies and nongovernmental organizations have been involved in the decades of this crusade. Yet, about 70 percent of Nigerians (about 84 million people) currently live in poverty, up from 42 percent in 1992, 46 percent in 1985, and 27 percent in 1980.

Income distribution and all social indicators have worsened. With the scourge of HIV/AIDS epidemic, life expectancy has plummeted. Child and maternal mortality rates are critically higher than the average for SSA and other developing countries, and the Human Development Report (UNDP 1999) ranks Nigeria 151 out of 174 countries. While incomes and social conditions continue to worsen, the population growth rate of 2.83 percent remains one of the highest in the world, thereby putting much pressures on resources and circumscribing development programs.

Furthermore, both Nigeria and most other SSA countries seem to be caught up in a complex web of vicious cycles that perpetuate poverty. The first group of factors includes low-equilibrium growth-savings-investment trap; that is, endemic poverty that is turning to be dynastic. It is also causing conflicts and circumscribes the weak governance institutions, low savings and investment, high dependency ratio, poor infrastructure, and income growth rates largely outstripped by population growth. For many of these countries, the size of the financing gap for sustainable development is enormous. Domestic savings need to rise but for head count poverty to fall consumption has to rise.

A second group of factor refers to the structural traps; that is, structural weaknesses of these economics that can potentially deter investible resources, and also limit the productivity of existing and future investment, such as geography and demography, weak and nonexistent markets, low capacity and capability, and production structure that is heavily dependent on primary commodities and lack diversification and competitiveness.

The third set of factors refers to leakages/decapitation; that is, terms of trade losses that offset 70 percent of the official development assistance (ODA) to SSA, while the loss of market shares cost SSA an annual income loss of about US$68 billion dollars per annum for the period 1972–97, huge debt service to export ratio that has sapped about 20 percent of median African country's exports since 1980, massive capital flight amounting to about 40 percent of private agents wealth or over US$225 billion, and huge brain drain estimated at about 30,000 African-trained professionals per annum.

Nigerian statistics are not any different from these and in many cases could be worse. For example, independent estimates variously put the stock of flight capital to be more than UUS$100 billion, more than twice the size of Nigeria's GDP and about three times the debt stock. Furthermore, the scourge of HIV/AIDS, with all the implications for social sector spending, loss of human capital and productivity, represents a major threat to development.

Finally, there is the problem of absorptive capacity. Africa and Nigeria's problem is as much a problem of the quantum of resources as it is that of efficiency of resource uptake and the absorptive capacity of the economy. Productivity of investment measured by the Incremental Output-Capital Ratio (IOCR) was less than half that in Asia for the period 1970–97, and from 1973 investment productivity declined from 27 percent to only 5 percent even with no significant change in investment levels

(World Bank 2000d).

Low capacity utilization of installed plant and equipment (around 30 percent for Nigeria) raises questions about the justification for new investment. In many countries, commercial banks are awash with excess liquidity, without much profitable investment outlets. At the heart of low absorptive capacity are issues related to the small size of the economies, availability of foreign exchange, risk and uncertainty, and mismanagement.

Evidently, poverty and inequality are deep and severe in Africa and Nigeria. But so are other challenges of underdevelopment.

Causes and Solution to Poverty and Inequality: The Debt Dimension

So what has debt to do with the situation described above? There is likely to be a strong correlation between debt and poverty, but the direction of causality depends on the specific time period of the debt accumulation. In the first instance, poverty and underdevelopment were the primary reasons why these countries resorted to external borrowing (the financing gap story). Analytically, countries borrow abroad for two broad reasons: macroeconomic reasons (higher investment, higher consumption (education/health)) or to finance transitory balance of payments deficits (to lower nominal interest rates abroad, lack of domestic long-term credit, or to circumvent hard budget constraints).

The underlying logic entails three phases of the debt cycle: In the first phase, debt grows in order to fill resource gaps. In the second phase the country generates resource surplus but probably not enough to offset interest payments. In the third phase it must generate enough surpluses to cover interest payments and amortization.

The peculiar Nigerian and African experience is that the countries have been trapped in the first two phases for decades. In the specific case of Nigeria, the structure of debt indicates that growth of Nigeria's debt has been mainly from the cumulating of unpaid arrears and less out of new borrowing. The fact of entrapment and cumulating of arrears is symptomatic of inherent difficulties in servicing the debt. Either that the debt incurred did not serve the purpose it was meant to serve, or that the problems of underdevelopment and poverty were so overwhelming that the generation of surpluses to pay back the debt was impossible.[3] Perhaps endemic poverty is the primary reason for poor countries to borrow unsustainably.

However, once the stock of debt accumulates, there are various channels through which debt could impact on poverty and inequality:

- Once an initial stock of debt grows to a certain threshold, servicing becomes a burden, and countries find themselves on the wrong side of the debt-Laffer curve, with debt crowding out investment and growth. Empirical evidence (Elbadawi, Ndulu, and Ndung'u, 1996) indicates that debt stock is a heavy tax on investment and growth. If, as we know, growth is good for poverty but debt is bad for growth, then it follows that debt overhang is bad for poverty. One might argue that in effect Nigeria has not been servicing its debt due and so debt reduction or cancellation is a mute point. Contractual debt service obligation for Nigeria is about US$3.7 billion per annum, and in the recent past it has been paying about US$1.5 to US$2 billion. So, de facto, Nigeria is already enjoying some debt relief (through rescheduling and accumulation of arrears) in the range of US$1.5–US$2 billion per annum. Add to that some further inflows in terms of ODA, and the net transfer of resources reduces further. However, there are still several channels through which both the existing stock of debt and the net transfers affect growth and poverty in Nigeria.

• One channel of impact of debt is the resource transfer effect (that is, debt servicing as a draw on resources. Actual debt service payment of US$1.5 to US$2 billion per annum (4 to 5 percent of GDP) is not trivial, and is larger than the combined federal government spending on the health, education, and poverty alleviation program. Ultimately, which sector suffers most depends on the relative distribution of power in society and on the relative organization/power of its beneficiaries and thus its lobbying power. There is the collective action problem here: beneficiaries of the social sector are diverse and organization is costly, and so it often gets short changed in the reallocation of spending.

• Compare the huge spending on the military (a powerful constituency) with that on the social sectors and the point becomes clear. It is not an accident that between 1980 and 1998 when debt accumulation intensified and debt service payments increased, primary and secondary school enrolment fell consistently, and tertiary education decayed. Were Nigeria to fully service its debt obligations (about 9 percent of GDP), then the net transfers would simply be enormous, and without an organized constituency to fight for it, the social sector might take the most heat.

Another point is that even where inflows significantly reduce the net transfers, it is the case that such inflows only imperfectly offset the outflows. First, much of the ODA inflows bypass national budgets, and thus are not within the control of national policymakers. Second, they are administered in such a manner that ensures effective round-tripping of the ODA back to the donor countries.

• The second channel of impact is involuntary or conditionality-induced policy changes owing to debt overhang. Debt rescheduling often requires a "certificate of good health" through a standby agreement with the International Monetary Fund (IMF). Potentially, the conditionality could help the poor through growth, but in practice it has not. While the counterfactual as to what would have happened without the policy conditionality is difficult to discern, there is a broad consensus that the conditionalities attached to much of these agreements have not been the best for poverty reduction.

The IMF has come to realize that while macroeconomic stability is essential for growth and poverty reduction, stabilization is not sustainable without directly addressing poverty. Consequently, it has renamed its Extended Structural Adjustment Facility (ESAF) Poverty Reduction and Growth Facility (PRGF). Frankly, the launching of the Comprehensive Development Framework (CDF) and the Poverty Reduction Strategy Programs (PRSPs) by the World Bank is a tacit acknowledgement that the old approaches have not worked. Not a few analysts are still skeptical about the efficacy of current approaches, but the hysteretic effects of previous conditionality-induced inappropriate policies persist, and not easily reversed.

For example, the fad in the 1980s through early 1990s was to de-emphasize tertiary education. After two decades of running down tertiary education, new approaches have now rediscovered the importance of higher education. Meanwhile, many of the universities and tertiary institutions have been ruined and would take quite a while to rebuild. This kind of conditionality-induced truncation of a development path is a direct cost of debt overhang. Many of such misguided policies persist, and ultimately hurt the poor. The leverage that donors have, and their willingness to interfere in the recipients' policy formation, is a critical lever that many donors do not want to relinquish.

• Third is the transactions intensity of debt and aid (O'Connell and Soludo 2001). Debtor countries could receive debt relief or net resource transfers in a variety of ways, but some are most costly to the recipients. One approach is to cancel the debt stock at the outset of the period, followed by grants on annual basis (of say US$X million per annum). The same ex post grant equivalent could be delivered through a sequence of rescheduling, outright grants, partial cancellations of new debt service due, and arrears accumulation, culminating in a large write off of remaining debt at the end of the period. A key issue in the debt overhang literature is that the latter arrangement is more costly to the borrower, even though the ex post discounted net transfer is identical.

In the context of the second approach, which is what happens in the case of Nigeria, none of the transactions affects net flows. In the extreme case, the intermittent Paris Club rescheduling, annual consultative group meetings, and constant dealings with bilateral and multilateral donors that underlie these flows simply represent a formalization of concessions already received. Nonrepayment is fully anticipated, all bargaining with donors is costly window dressing, and net flows—revealed *ex post* but known in advance to participants—capture all that matters. The economic impact of these transactions is familiar (Agenor and Montiel 1996). The process of debt rescheduling is bureaucratically costly. In 1998, Tanzanian bureaucrats were said to have written more than 2,700 reports to donors. Across Africa, the average senior civil servant spends about 50 percent of his or her time dealing with donors. In Nigeria currently, more resources seem to be devoted to managing external debt than to managing poverty alleviation programs.

Furthermore, debt overhang creates uncertainty about the status of upcoming debt service claims and the timing and amount of concessions. It, therefore, creates policy uncertainty, because policymakers cannot plan over a reasonably longer time horizon without knowing in advance how much of debt relief will be forthcoming.

• Finally, there is the signaling effect of debt on investment, in so far as the stock remains on the books, it represents a potential tax on future effort. First, rapid export growth will likely lead to reduced official flows or increased service payments, thereby constituting a tax on efforts. Second, it signals uncertainty about future economic policies, and also indicates potential future increases in domestic taxes to effect the financial transfers to service debt. Investors therefore, exercise their option to wait.

Ajay Chhibber, former lead economist, West Africa region of the World Bank, has estimated the effect of debt overhang on investment and growth in Nigeria (Chhibber and Pahwa 1993, pp. 15 to 16):

A 50 percent reduction in the debt stock in 1986 to accompany the introduction of the SAP would have had substantial benefits in the form of growth and recovery of private investment. These benefits would have come from a substantial reduction in the foreign exchange premium, which would have dropped on average from 33 percent to 23 percent during the 1987–91 period.

GDP growth would have averaged 2.9 percent higher rising from 5.2 percent per annum to 7.3 percent per annum. Private investment would have recovered very rapidly rising by well over 20 percent per annum so that the private investment ratio would have risen to average 7 percent of GDP instead of 5 percent of GDP in the 1987–91 period. These simulations show the powerful drag on Nigeria from the debt overhang. The cost of this debt overhang has amounted to over 2 percent per annum in GDP growth. These benefits can be realized with a policy cum debt relief program in the future. Based on current projections on labor force growth of around 2.7 percent per annum the Nigerian economy is projected to grow at around 1 to 2 percent per annum under the current policy stance and with the existing debt overhang. They also show that with a carefully constructed policy program coupled with debt relief, the economy could be growing at 6 to 7 percent per annum instead of at 1 to 2 percent per annum where it would barely keep pace with population growth.

So for Nigeria it is not hypothetical whether or not debt overhang hurts. There is evidence that it hurts very much. It is because of these negative impacts of debt overhang that many analysts conclude that the best option is to cancel the debt of the heavily indebted countries. There are other arguments for debt relief, of course. Some of the arguments border on morality, and others on the legitimacy of the debt.

However, some analysts raise the moral hazard argument, pointing out that a repayment of the debt would amount to rewarding the irresponsible lending behavior of the creditors. It is argued that the creditors knew the conditions of these economies, that the money was not being used for the purposes meant and yet kept on lending. In the case of international finance institutions (IFIs) there is the phenomenon of loan pushing, where officials are rewarded on the basis of the amount of credit they are able to dole out, regardless of the risks involved. In this regard, there are questions about the legitimacy of debts incurred by corrupt dictatorships such as Mobutu in Zaire or the military in Nigeria. There are, however, controversies as to whether the IFIs can afford to cancel the debt.

Nigeria's case is, however, different. It does not owe much to the IFIs, but more than 70 percent of its debt is to the Paris Club. Can the rich countries afford to cancel the debt, especially in the light of unprecedented prosperity and post-Cold War peace dividend? For many analysts, including the former U.S. Treasury Secretary Larry Summers (See Box 3 in the Annex), debt cancellation is not only sound economics but it is also affordable by the rich countries. The only stumbling block is the lack of political will to do the right thing.

Besides, there is the moral argument as well. Just think about the fact that by 2020, Nigeria would have paid back US$5 for every US$1 that she borrowed. So far, on a debt of about US$13 billion, Nigeria has already paid US$21 billion over the years in debt service, and yet the capitalization of arrears and penalties still leaves the country with a debt stock of US$28 billion. Someone might ask whether US$21 billion in past payments is not enough for the US$13 billion borrowed?

Current Initiatives: An Assessment

There is a global consensus that the old approaches to debt, poverty, and inequality have not worked. The creditors have also accepted debt relief as a strategy for poverty reduction, but the extent and nature of relief are contentious. The key elements of the policy thrusts of the mainstream "old" and "new" approaches are summarized in World Bank (1996; 2000b), and we compare them in Box 1.

Box 1: Comparison of First and Second Generations of Poverty Reduction Measures

World Development Report, 1990: Poverty	World Development Report, 2000: Attacking Poverty
• Broad-based economic growth, including five key components: (i) providing necessary framework for broad-based (labor-intensive) growth, with emphasis on agriculture, transportation and social services; (ii) ensuring access to essential assets such as land and credit; (iii) increasing the productivity of the poor through investment in basic education and health, agricultural extension, and business training; (iv) making sure markets work for the poor, building and maintaining rural infrastructure, and lifting unnecessary and burdensome regulations such licensing and start-up taxes for small firms; and (iv) overcoming discrimination against the poor.	• Promoting Opportunity: Expanding economic opportunity for poor people by stimulating overall economic growth and by building up their assets (such as land and education) and increasing the returns on these assets, through a combination of market and nonmarket actions. • Facilitating empowerment: Making state institutions more accountable and responsive to poor people, strengthening the participation of poor people in political processes and local decision-making, and removing the social barriers that result from distinctions of gender, ethnicity, race, religion, and social status.
• Developing the Human Capital of the Poor, including early childhood development, primary education, and education for girls. • Safety Nets, including analysis and design of safety nets for the sick, the old, the disabled, those in the poorest regions, and those suffering from temporary economic setbacks.	• Enhancing security: Reducing poor people's vulnerability to ill health, economic shocks, crop failure, policy-induced dislocations, natural disasters, and violence as well as helping them cope with adverse shocks when they occur. A big part of this is ensuring that effective safety nets are in place to mitigate the impacts of personal and national calamities.

What is the difference between the two reports in terms of policy direction? Except for the greater emphasis on accountability of public institutions and participation of the poor in decision making and management of their affairs, the new approach is, in substance, a rehearsal of the old one.

Both approaches focus essentially on the national (country-based) efforts. As the World Bank (1999, p. 1) observes, the new framework under the PRSPs is "designed to promote progress towards the international development goals for reducing poverty in its various dimensions, on a country basis." Although the World Bank (2000b) recognizes the important point that "action at the local and national levels is not enough," its proposals for "global action" remain mere suggestions, since they are not yet part of the World Bank programs.

Another important element of the new approach is the promise of "increased" new money, especially through debt relief under the Enhanced HIPC initiative. Such a debt relief, expected to total about US$20 billion in net present value terms (for countries covered by the Special Program of Assistance to Africa), is to be tied to poverty alleviation. In the new approach donors are expected to monitor spending of resources freed under the Enhanced HIPC to ensure that they are directed toward poverty strategies as developed under the PRSPs. In principle, this strategy is laudable, but some critics have argued that the Enhanced HIPC does not go far enough in addressing the fundamental issues related to poverty reduction. Besides, Nigeria is not a HIPC country and thus does not benefit from a HIPC-type debt relief.[4]

Toward an Exit Strategy: The Nigerian Domestic Agenda

A sustainable debt strategy is one that over a reasonable time horizon ensures that the country/region escapes from debt and aid dependence as well as the traps of pervasive poverty and inequality. So far, 50 years of aid and debt, as well as nearly one dozen special development initiatives on Africa (mostly under the aegis of the United Nations), and dozens of Nigeria's national programs on poverty have not produced much results. Poverty is on the rise, and inequality is deepening. If Nigeria succeeds in preventing an escalation in poverty, then it would have about 170 million poor people in 25 years time. Even this target of just preventing an escalation is proving a difficult one, if current trends are anything to go by.

Ideas about the new aid and debt relationships in the post-Cold War era are still evolving. But one thing is certain: It is no longer business as usual. Development finance, especially the ODA is on a precipitous decline. The international NGO community and poor countries are crying foul. However, aid is not a lifetime entitlement. Just like the industrial countries are reforming their welfare system to encourage a transition from welfare to workfare, so, too, does a country like Nigeria need an exit strategy to escape the entrapment of debt and poverty. The first and most important locus of such a strategy is the national level, a national agenda.

Such a national agenda must have key elements and address some fundamental questions. First, the good news is the creation of the Debt Management Office (DMO), and soon we should know precisely how much we owe, and have a system for timely tracking of such a debt. It is also a system that takes full cognizance of our domestic debt, which is also ballooning. Second, such a strategy must set a reasonable time horizon within which the country expects to complete the exit. We need to know how much resources are required to execute this strategy and where the money will come from. What is the best option for Nigeria in terms of debt relief? Should Nigeria borrow externally, when and for what purpose? What reforms are necessary to ensure efficiency and effectiveness of resource use? How do we mobilize idle resources and exploit Nigeria's growth reserves? Which international initiatives should Nigeria latch on to to ensure the best terms for its debt and future aid? The questions are many and answers too broad to be fully explained here.

Policy Direction: How Much Would It Cost?

It is important to underscore at the outset that both the Obasanjo's Economic Policy Direction, 1999–2003, and the National Policy on Poverty Eradication say all the right things in terms of ambitious targets and instruments. Were these targets achievable through a magic wand, Nigeria might achieve the international target of reducing poverty incidence by half in 2015 within Obasanjo's presidency.[5] All indications, however, point in the opposite direction. What is missing is the full costing of the programs and projects; that is, just how much money would be required to implement them and where would the resources come from?

Quite a lot of money is involved. Given the growth elasticity of poverty, the growth rate required to achieve the international development goal of halving poverty in 2015 is 7 to 8 percent . Also, given the level of efficiency in the economy (measured by the Incremental Capital-Output Ratio (ICOR), the level of investment requirement to achieve that growth is enormous, more than 30 percent. The national savings rate is about 15 percent. Assuming net inflows of about 5 percent (larger than historical trend) this still leaves a resource gap of at least 10 percent of GDP per annum.

Add to this the cost of targeted interventions to redress poverty, such as programs in health, education, and rural infrastructure. The East Asian countries are said to have grown rich because of their spectacular investment in these areas. Assuming Nigeria benchmarks its spending on these sectors (as percentage of GDP) to the East Asian levels when they were at similar stage of development, it could translate into a disproportionately large share of government budget. The health sector is complicated by the scourge of HIV/AIDS, which, under current under funding, costs the average African country some 3 percent of GDP per annum. Assume that Nigerian government devotes 10 percent of GDP to health expenditure, that would still amount to merely USUS$30 per capita per annum, the cost of a meal in a rich country restaurant.

So there are serious resource constraints, and Nigeria would need all the debt relief that it can get. Currently, Nigeria pays US$1.5 to US$2 billion per annum in debt service, out of the US$3.7 billion due. The rest is rescheduled. Effectively, a debt relief that comes by way of outright cancellation of the debt stock by creditors would release additional US$1.7 to US$2.2 billion per annum. With about 80 million Nigerians in poverty, this translates to about USUS$21 per poor person per year, or about 5 cents per day. This might sound miniscule. However, if this amount is devoted to health and education, it would more than triple the budget for these sectors. Over a 10 year period it would mean an additional US$15 to US$20 billion in these sectors, and properly managed, could lift millions out of poverty.

Efficiency is Perhaps More Important
The financing problem of Nigeria and African countries goes beyond the quantum of resources. If the quantum of investible resources were the only problem and if the predictions of the Harrod-Domar model held, then many of the African LDCs should have graduated into middle and high income economies. Zambia, in particular, should have been a US$22,000 per capita economy. Needless to add that despite the massive aid to Zambia, it remains a US$700 per capita economy in 1999, with little structural transformation and endemic poverty. There are still critical questions about the absorptive capacity of these economics as well as the efficiency of resource use. For example, on the average a dollar of spending in the health sector has generated only 12 cents of benefits (World Bank 2000d). Perhaps the first order of business is to undertake reforms to ensure that a dollar of spending gets at least 80 cents of benefits. This will be a lot.

In Nigeria, economywide capacity utilization rate (industry and agriculture) is about 30 percent. Most installed capacity is idle, and money is only a part of the explanation. The main reason has to do with several self-inflicted constraints, and poor institutional and administrative set up that raise the transaction costs and constrain enterprise. Indeed, just raising the capacity utilization rate from 30 percent to say 70 percent can create millions of jobs and lift many out of poverty.

Borrowing to Finance Investment and Poverty Reduction
The preceding argument would counsel against recourse to borrowing in the short to medium terms. Answers to two questions would help to make this position clearer. First, what happened to the nearly US$300 billion in oil revenues in the last three decades? We know that much of it was wasted and stolen, with the average Nigerian getting impoverished. What did we do with the various oil windfalls during the Shagari and Babangida regimes? Second, what did Nigeria achieve with the billions of dollars it borrowed in the past? Not much either. For example, a survey of some 145 projects funded by US$14 billion revealed that about 18 of them never even got started, and yet the loans were fully drawn, and many others remained uncompleted, and of those that were completed, many were nonperforming.

More fundamentally, the expectations that these projects would contribute to poverty reduction through employment and growth did not happen. These are the debts Nigeria is still servicing. Do we have basis to expect that things are now different? Not yet. The government is making efforts to fight corruption, and also reform certain institutions, but we are still very far from a framework to guarantee maximum utilization of resources.

If our past were any guide to the future we would suggest that the government places a moratorium on domestic and external borrowing for at least the next 5 to 10 years, and this should apply to all tiers of government. The current frenzy with borrowing and spending by the state governments must be checked before the current regimes bankrupt the future generations. During the moratorium period, a major effort should be made toward reengineering the institutions to ensure maximum efficiency of a dollar of spending, be it an oil windfall, a debt relief, or a borrowed fund.

So, let us first of all work on efficiency. And make no mistake about it: Nigerians need democracy dividends very quickly. However, reckless borrowing and spending to satisfy short-term political interests but jeopardize the long-term economic interests of the poor is not the way to do it. A key issue in addressing issues of efficiency of resource use will be research to understand the level and determinants of the economy's absorptive capacity. We need to understand the size and structure of spending that can be undertaken without dislocating the macro balance. Paradoxically, a major challenge during this period of oil boom is how to restrain the state from "excessive" spending beyond the capacity of state institutions to manage them effectively. What Nigeria cannot afford is a repeat of the history of wasteful spending.

Beyond the need to address issues of efficiency, a second reason for resisting any further borrowing is to signal the dawn of a new era. Nigeria suffers from a reputational problem, and government credibility is badly tarnished by past behavior. The hysteresis of such past behavior lingers. The government needs to send a strong signal that it will no longer be business as usual. Given the coun-

Debt, Poverty and Inequality

try's abundant natural resources, Nigeria should never have had anything to do with debt. Having been trapped in it for decades now, the government needs to signal a strong commitment to redress the mistakes of the past.

During the moratorium period, the government should:

- Exploit all options to secure maximum debt relief possible, including the option of complete debt cancellation[6]
- Strengthen its capacity for public resource management, including debt (budgetary and debt management), as well as effective government /think tanks/civil society/NGO partnerships to ensure effective monitoring, research and analysis, as well as oversight
- Strengthen capacities for resource management at the local and state governments. Most of the poor live in rural areas, and ideally the major chunk of poverty alleviation programs should be pursued at the local government and community levels. This would also have made a case for allocating more resources to the lower tiers of government. Unfortunately, the capacity to effectively administer the programs and manage resources at that level is sorely lacking
- Undertake up-to-date poverty assessment
- Accept only pure grants, and not even IDA loans
- Ensure macro stability (lower and stable prices, stable but competitive exchange rate, and lower real interest rate), which helps the poor more
- Develop a national aid strategy to domesticate

foreign aid and ensure true transfer of technical assistance. In the 1980s and 1990s, Africa received about US$4 billion per annum in technical assistance, funding about 100,000 expatriate consultants. What capacity was built? Relatively none. Currently, as part of the new aid relationships, many countries are untying much of their aid, and African countries (including Nigeria) need to devise national strategies to take full advantages of the new initiatives

• Enact a strict law guiding foreign borrowing, and specifically spelling out the purpose and institutional mechanisms for evaluation, monitoring, and oversight, including penalties for nonperformance. It is too easy and naive to simply say that projects for foreign borrowing must pass a cost-benefit evaluation. Of course, all the failed projects and programs of the past passed such tests. A new institutional structure involving the executive, parliament, and civil society is needed to negotiate and administer such new borrowings in the long term.

Can Nigeria afford to do without borrowing in the next 5 to 10 years? Yes, Nigeria can afford not to borrow a cent (domestically or externally) in the next five years. Of course, Nigeria has not been borrowing much in the recent past, only that it has not been servicing its debt. The case for resisting borrowing is even stronger now, especially if the oil windfall is better managed, and if the donors do not hassle the government into transferring the windfall to them rather than investing it at home.

Second, the amounts being borrowed (few hundred millions at most) are simply too small to make any significant difference. Indeed, relative to the resources being wasted and mismanaged, the potential new borrowing is very small but the consequences, conditionality, and transactions intensity are grave. Moreover, there are huge resource reserves waiting to be exploited: targeting Nigeria's private assets abroad, investing the privatization proceeds in a trust fund for poverty alleviation, and removing the self-inflicted constraints to unleash a true private sector-led development.

Targeting Private Assets Abroad
Nigeria's problem is essentially that of a mismatch of assets; that is, private sector accumulates massive assets abroad while the government owns the liability (debt). Private assets abroad (mainly capital flight and looted funds) are estimated to be at least twice the size of GDP, and more than three times the national debt. With the right kinds of policies and incentives, many of these asset holders could be induced to repatriate them back. Assume for the sake of illustration that such assets amount to about US$100 billion. If only the interest earnings on those assets are repatriated, the economy would benefit from an additional annual injection of some US$ 10 billion (or about 25 percent of GDP). Indeed, if only Nigeria can put in place mechanisms to attract back 25 percent of flight capital, and discourage new ones from fleeing the country, Nigeria may not need foreign resources in the near future. The problem is to create such an environment.

Tangential to the issue of attracting flight capital is

how to deal with the looting by corrupt officials. One approach is to continue the campaign to recover the money or materials. That is a laudable effort. The problem, however, is how much can the country reasonably expect to get back and over what period? Much of the "successes" so far are with dead officials. Another approach is to draw a thick line against the past, and try the Korean-style "amnesty" to the looters, provided they can invest them in productive activities within the country.

These are no easy choices and ultimately the decision has to be a political one. The point here is that the country must have a strategy, and a long-term plan of not only how to get the monies back but more importantly how to invest them.

Trust Fund for Privatization Proceeds
Another potential permanent source of revenue to the government is privatization of public enterprises. Politicians often have short time-horizons and under pressure to do something "now." If care is not taken, the revenue from privatization could be frittered away as current consumption. A more prudent approach is to set up a trust fund and invest the proceeds in the capital market (bonds and stocks), and use the annual returns to augment government revenues in perpetuity. One potential use for the trust fund money is to devote the proceeds entirely to spending on the social sector. For Nigeria, the proceeds of such privatization are expected to run into billions of dollars, and it is conceivable that the annual returns could be multiples of any new transfers from Overseas Development Assistance (ODA) or new borrowings.

A Strategy to Boost Productivity
Nigeria must implement a strategy to fundamentally overhaul and unleash the supply side (productivity) of the economy to create an environment for competitive private enterprise to flourish. Currently, about two third of productive resources in Nigeria are either unemployed or underemployed. A creative use of the oil windfall as well as sound economic policies can unleash a momentum for sustainable development that will lift millions out of poverty through private enterprise. In particular, Nigeria should fully maximize the potentials offered under the U.S. Government Africa Growth Opportunities Act (AGOA) and new European Union-Africa-Caribbean-Pacific Agreement (Cotonou Agreement). Furthermore, it should lobby to be included in the new European Union trade concessions to the LDCs the so-called "everything but arms" that allows LDCs to export everything but arms into the European Union duty free.

In conclusion, it must be reiterated that Nigeria has enormous potential for a new beginning. It needs all the debt relief that it can get. More importantly, it needs to do a lot to put its house in order, so as to ensure the most efficient use of current and future resources.

Toward an Exit Strategy: Africa and the Global Agenda

For the poorest countries, actions at the local and national levels are not enough for sustainable poverty eradication in a world of globalization (World Bank 2000b). For a comprehensive attack on poverty, a global action plan is required.[7] No doubt, there has been no shortage of global agenda, and, in particular, there has been about a dozen special international initiatives on Africa since 1980. However, thus far they have not worked. Poverty and inequality continue to rise. And there is a broad consensus that a global response is required, but disparate ideas remain on how to do so. Our argument here is that the world is in need of a fundamental rethinking of the governance structure in the light of the increasing economic interdependence.

A critical point often not appreciated is that the ramifications of poverty that create "dynastic" localized poverty traps in particular regions of the world are intricately related to the nature of the globalization process. Castells (1998) provides a lucid statement of this phenomenon:

> Everywhere, they are growing in number, and increasing in visibility, as the selective triage of informational capitalism, and the political breakdown of the welfare state, intensify social exclusion. In the current historical context, the rise of the Fourth World is inseparable from the rise of informational, global capitalism....Whatever the reason, for these territories, and for the people trapped in them, a downward spiral of poverty, then dereliction, finally irrelevance, operates until or unless a countervailing force, including people's revolt against their condition, reverses the trend. This is unless there is a change in the laws that govern the universe of informational capitalism, since, unlike cosmic forces, purposive human action can change the rules of social structure,

including those inducing social exclusion.

No doubt, poor countries have a lot to gain from the globalizing world, not least is the potential catch-up effects of tapping into the networked global information and technological highways. They can also benefit from trade and international finance. Most African economies are already deeply integrated into the global economy, albeit at the wrong end of the stick (aid dependency, highest capital flight of any region, massive brain drain, and trade in primary commodities buffeted by volatile and declining terms of trade).

A point that is little understood, however, is that globalization is also one of the major causes of deepening poverty in Africa. Two major factors make globalization central to an understanding of the poverty story. First, is the insight from the endogenous growth theory that initial conditions matter, and that path dependence is valid. Second, is the asymmetry with which the policies and programs that shape globalization treat productive assets and people.

Under globalization, the productive assets—financial capital and high-skilled human capital—are allowed to be mobile across boundaries, whereas the population at large is confined to geographic boundaries. These two factors therefore work in a mutually reinforcing manner to create "dynastic" poverty traps in some regions and prosperity in others. Given poorer initial conditions, there is the "push" factor in the poor countries, which drive away productive assets to flee in search of higher or safer returns.

Conversely, there is the "pull" factor in the richer countries, which ensures an increasing concentration of global financial capital, and human skills in places with a head start. Such leakages or spillovers (currently on an unprecedented scale) create multiple equilibria in the global economy, with low-equilibrium, poverty traps coexisting with higher equilibrium, and prosperous havens (Soludo 2000a, 2000b).

Africa's experience in the last 40 years bears out the above characterization. Various estimates of capital flight indicate that private agents in Africa hold about 40 percent of their wealth abroad (compared to about 4 percent for Asians), and about 30,000 skilled African professionals migrate to the West every year. In essence, Africa's efforts at savings and higher skill development represent a subsidy to the West. The terms of trade losses offset about 70 percent of the ODA, while the loss of market shares in international trade has cost Africa some US$68 billion per annum between 1972 and 1997 (World Bank et al, 2000d).

The global trading regime, especially the agricultural subsidy in the West also adversely affects the competitive advantage of African peasant farmers, thereby further impoverishing them. Preferential regional arrangements—North American Free Trade Association with Mexico, and European Union with North Africa and Central Europe—greatly help the beneficiaries but also harm the more distant, poorer regions by drawing away foreign direct investment and trade. Add to this the fact that the cartelization of global shipping ensures that trading routes linking marginal traders (poorest regions) to the major markets tend to be uncompetitive and expensive (Sachs 2000b).

In addition, some diseases have now become African in character and magnitude—malaria, HIV/AIDS, and tuberculosis. Africa is also far too behind in technological development, especially those required to cater for its unique tropical environment, and in an era of breathtaking technological changes.

Africa is at risk of permanently remaining behind.[8] The challenges are simply too overwhelming to permit meaningful progress in today's competitive, globalizing world, and, as stated earlier, even the continent's current star performer—Uganda—is estimated to remain an LDC until 2020. Not surprisingly, poverty remains pervasive, even after two decades of market-oriented adjustment programs. With nearly 50 percent of the population living in absolute poverty, 5 percent of GDP growth rate is required just to prevent the number of poor people from increasing, and more than 7 percent annual growth rate is needed to significantly reduce poverty in the longer run.

Even with the East Asian efficiency levels, this would require an investment rate of about 30 percent, a large number compared with the average savings rate of 13 percent in the 1990s (World Bank 2000d). Tables 1 and 2 show estimates of growth and resource requirements by sub-regions in Africa. Currently, GDP growth rate is barely 3 percent, ODA is falling in real and nominal terms, and service payments on accumulated debt is greater than most African governments' budget for the social sector. With poverty on the rise, it is little surprise that civil wars and socio-political unrest, as well as violent crimes have been escalating in recent years in the region (with all the added burden of refugees, for example).

Table 1. Africa: Growth Requirements for 50% Poverty Reduction by 2015

Africa Region	Per Capita Monthly Expenditure (1985 PPP)	Estimated Gini Coefficient (%)	1998 GDP Share (%)	1998 population share (%)	Growth Elasticity of Poverty	Required per capita Growth (%)	Population Growth Rate (%)	Required GDP Growth Rate (%)
North	122	37.0	40.26	21.7	-1.11	3.60	2.0	5.60
West	53	43.0	17.23	29.2	-0.85	4.71	2.90	7.61
Nigeria	(56)	(45)	(8.11)	(15.7)	(0.71)	(5.63)	(2.9)	(8.53)
Central	77	42.3	5.14	3.9	-1.02	3.90	2.80	6.70
East	38	43.4	7.85	30.9	-0.74	5.40	2.70	8.12
Southern	90	47.4	29.52	14.3	-1.05	3.80	2.40	6.20
Total/Ave (SSA)	76 (65)	44 (43)	100 (59.74)	100 (78.3)	-0.92 (0.95)	4.19 (4.39)	2.60 (2.77)	6.79 (7.16)

Source: UN-ECA, 1999. *Economic Report on Africa*

How does one begin to tackle poverty in this circumstance without a comprehensive framework that integrates the domestic and global agenda? As Castells (1998) argues, unless there is a change in the laws governing global information capitalism, it is not conceivable how these countries could escape from the throes of poverty. But the "purposive human action" envisaged by Castells cannot happen without a new understanding and conviction of the interconnections between the new global economy and localized poverty traps.

Such an understanding requires two elements. First, poverty eradication needs to be conceived as an international public good, which should be collectively provided. With the benefits of globalization accruing to an increasingly diminishing number of people in the world (two thirds of humanity left behind), the current system is largely unsustainable. Just as the welfare state and the various social insurance mechanisms at the national level prevented the realization of Karl Marx's prediction of proletarian revolution against industrial capitalism, so also would a system of global social insurance/transfer mechanism prevent the realization of Castells' prediction of a "violent revolt" against the global information capitalism.

Table 2. Required Growth and Investment Rates to Halve Poverty in Africa by 2015

Sub-Region	Required GDP Growth Rate (%)	Incremental Capital-Output Ratio (ICOR)	Required Investment Rate	Current Investment Rate	Investment Gap (Extra Investment required as % of GDP)
North	5.60	3.8	21.3		
West	7.61	4.8	36.5	17.6	18.9
Central	6.70	7.3	48.9	20.0	28.9
East	8.12	5.6	45.5	14.6	30.9
South	6.20	6.1	37.8	17.6	20.2
Africa Average	6.79	5.0	33.0	20.5	12.5
Sub-Saharan Africa	7.16	5.8	40.0	17.4	22.6

Source: UN-ECA, 1999, *Economic Report on Africa*

In essence, eradication of localized poverty traps around the world is not just a humanitarian concern (as it is currently couched) but an economic imperative. Apart from sustainability of the entire system, poverty eradication allows more than two thirds of humanity increasingly left behind to contribute to world economic prosperity, and everyone benefits from such prosperity.[9] If basic capability—education, health, and nutrition—is central to productivity at the national level, it is even more so for the global economy. Empirical estimates of the potential impact of productivity improvements of the world's poorest populations on global output/income are needed.

Already, as a consequence of this growing poverty and helplessness, the global criminal economy experiences phenomenal growth, and is now worth over US$1.5 trillion per annum (that is, trade in narcotics, prostitution, human trafficking, fraud, violent crimes, and mercenary private armies).[10]

Second, is that the interconnectivity between poverty

and global information capitalism requires a global governance structure to design and administer global social insurance and transfer mechanisms that go beyond the current design and mandate of the multilateral institutions.[11] It is perhaps not controversial that some global actions are required (though not necessarily for the reasons stated above) as the various editions of UNDP's *Human Development Report*, and recently the *World Development Report 2000/2001* (World Bank 2000b) and World Bank(2000d) make clear.

The U.S. Africa Growth and Opportunity Act, the European Union-Africa-Caribbean-Pacific agreements, and the new European Union "everything but arms" are demonstrations of increasing understanding and political support of the idea that Africa and the LDCs need special and differential treatments. It is also not controversial that more resources are needed. That is what all the proposals for debt relief and calls for increased aid budgets are all about.

What is perhaps controversial is the question of just how much resources are required, and more so, about how to mobilize such resources. Our central argument here is that a missing element in the poverty eradication proposals and policies is the inability to come to terms with the quantum of resources required, and to design mechanisms to ensure mandatory transfers of such resources to the poorest locations.

First, the absolute quantum of resources is the most important constraint to poverty eradication. There is emerging consensus that Africa needs a significant growth rate (at least 7 percent compared to the current 3 percent) to make a dent on poverty and that even at the

East Asian efficiency levels, such a growth rate would need an investment rate of at least 30 percent. Thus, on growth issues alone, Africa needs extra annual investment rates of at least 15 percent of GDP, which in current dollars amounts to about US$50 billion in additional investment per annum. Sachs (2000b, p. 100) estimates that tackling the lethal diseases of malaria, HIV/AIDS, tuberculosis, measles, diarrhea, and other infectious diseases, would require about US$10 billion per year. Compare this US$60 billion in additional spending with the less than US$20 billion in multilateral lending and FDI into Africa.

Furthermore, investment in education and health is not estimated. It would have been more helpful if the World Social and Sustainable Development Summit (WSSD) had estimated the magnitude of resources required to achieve its various goals and clearly identify the sources. No doubt, as percentage of GDP, Africa spends more on education than Asian and Latin American developing countries (World Bank 2000d, p. 113). But the key issue is the absolute magnitude of resources relative to need.

Consider Ethiopia with US$100 per capita in 1999: Assuming that it spends 50 percent of its GDP on health, that would be a paltry US$50 per person per year. The point here is that even though efforts should be intensified to improve the efficiency of resource use, the absolute size of the resource base is such that some of the percentages and cross-country comparisons may be misleading.

Another issue is the 20/20 initiative. Again, take the Ethiopian example. Given the size of ODA to Ethiopia and its national budget, even if the 20/20 initiative is met, this would still be too paltry to scratch the gigantic social problems in the country. Matters become complicated when we factor in the facts that terms of trade losses offset about 70 percent of ODA, and that most African countries spend more on debt service payments than the total spending on the social sector, health and education, combined.

Against this background, the Enhanced HIPC initiative certainly represents progress, but a critical rethinking is required to make the initiative serve the interests of the poor (See Box 2).

Perhaps the most portent challenge to thinking through the reforms is how to mobilize and disburse the required resources. The current system depends on the altruism of donors, and since the end of the Cold War, such altruism has waned, and ODA has been falling despite all the appeals to good conscience."[12] Even though the net resource flows is still positive for Africa, the character of the flows make a fundamental difference for the social sector.

Box 2: Making the Enhanced HIPC Work for the Poor

The Enhanced HIPC (EH) re-opens the international official discussion about the HIPC debt crisis. Unfortunately, the EH leaves in place many of the serious flaws of the original HIPC initiative of 1996. While the new initiative aims at more "ambitious" debt reduction targets than the 1996 HIPC initiative, the basic problem remains that the new standards are as arbitrary as the old ones. Both initiatives focus mainly on the relationship of debt to exports, even though debt-to-export ratios have little if anything to do with the real ability of governments to meet urgent social needs while servicing debts,

Even though the net resource transfers tend to be positive, the debt servicing system is fundamentally flawed. First, and most urgently, the net resource transfers are not large enough to enable the HIPC governments to meet basic health and education needs of the population. Second, the bilateral grants do not neatly offset the heavy burden of debt servicing, even if they appear to do so in formal accounting. The debt burden falls heavily on the budget, and therefore on line ministries (such as the Ministry of Health) while grants frequently finance extra-budgetary activities established by the donors. Third, the process of offsetting heavy debt payments with grants and new loans is highly unstable and erratic. There is no guarantee that new grants will fill the fiscal void left behind by the heavy debt servicing; indeed sometimes there is a self-fulfilling collapse of fiscal resources. The instability, unpredictability, and time-consuming nature of these rollover mechanisms contribute to the incapacity of HIPC governments and the international community to formulate long-term solutions to the pressing social crises in the HIPC countries.

The revised HIPC program should reestablish the fiscal base for meeting the urgent social needs confronting the HIPC countries. This should be done in the following ways: for almost all HIPCs, we should recognize the need for significant, and increased, net resource transfers for the foreseeable future; to bring about these increased net resource transfers, debt servicing on old debts should be cancelled, while maintaining or increasing the flow of grants and loans; to the maximum extent possible, new transfers should come in the form of grants and concessional loans (ODA), rather than commercial loans; debts owed to bilateral creditors should be forgiven in their entirety in most cases, upon demonstration of need, in the context of a process that aims to channel the budgetary saving to urgent social needs; debts owed to the IBRD (nonconcessional World Bank financing) should be forgiven as well; IDA loans need to be forgiven only in the unusual circumstances that IDA debt servicing is imposing large net resource costs on a particular country, or is likely to do so in the next few years; ESAF and standby loan repayments should be forgiven, as net repayments to the IMF represent a growing burden on the HIPCs; in cases where the private-sector debt is a substantial burden on economic development, these private sector debts should be substantially forgiven as well.

If bilateral loans and grants remained unchanged, while debt servicing on public and publicly guaranteed debts owed to the Paris Club, IBRD, and IMF, and other multilateral creditors are forgiven, the result would be a sizeable increase in net resource transfers to the

> HIPC countries, on the order of US$5 billion per year, and a substantial decrease in the long-term debt stock, on the order of over 60 percent of the existing debt stock.
>
> In the future, decisions over the extent of debt relief should be made in view of a detailed assessment of real social needs. UN agencies that specialize in critical social areas should play a decisive role in the process of assisting the HIPCs, working under the leadership of the HIPC governments to prepare "social audits" that can be the basis for a revised and revived strategy on meeting urgent social needs. NGOs involved in social services should also be encouraged to provide inputs to the deliberative process. The key UN agencies would include the World Health Organization, the UN Children's Fund, the Joint UN Program on HIV-AIDS, the World Food Program, and the Food and Agricultural Organization.
>
> Source: Center for International Development (1999).

First, the outflows come mostly from government budgets, while the bulk of the inflows are delivered through largely uncoordinated donor projects which bypass the national budget. Second, the inflows are erratic and unpredictable, because they depend on the political expediencies of the donors. Also, the multiple donors, with multiple accounting and administrative standards, impose heavy transaction costs on the recipients. All these make ODA ineffective.

Our view is that only a system of mandatory transfers from the richest to the poorest regions of the world can provide the framework for tackling poverty on a comprehensive basis. While many people agree that such an arrangement would be superior to the current ODA, their only concern is its political feasibility, at least in the short to medium term.

Our response is that such concerns should not prevent us from creative thinking. But even on feasibility, we note that the proposal is not too far from commitments already freely made by the OECD countries on ODA. For example, such a mandatory transfer mechanism could entail the "enforcement" of the agreed ODA/GDP ratios, or it might entail setting new targets.

Alternatively, some other sources of funding could be explored Soludo (2000a, 2000b) and Sachs (2001), for example, has variously shown what US$8 or US$10 per American (or per OECD citizen) per year could achieve for the poorest countries. There is certainly room for creative thinking on how to source the additional funding.[13] More so, there is also room to debate the best delivery mechanism and conditionalities to be attached to it, whether as pure grants or grants plus concessionary lending (ODA). The key principle is a global agenda that ensures predictable transfers of needed resources to lift all locations out of poverty.

Two other elements of the global response are needed. First, there is need for an international law that makes stolen money unsafe anywhere in the world. So far, the global system functions in a hypocritical manner with regards to fight against corruption. A caricature of the prevailing rule, especially as practiced by the industrial countries reads like this: "Corruption is bad at the national level, but if you manage to loot and bring it to our economies, we will help you to safe keep it."

Indeed, if a global transparency and fight against corruption leads to the repatriation of looted wealth back to their owners—citizens of the poorest countries—many of them can write a check and repay their debt in one day, and still have surplus for other development programs. Without an international response, the extent of poverty and risks in these developing countries would guarantee that capital will continue to flee into the richer economies.

The second element is trade. First, the subsidies to agriculture in the West need fundamental reforms. Second, the industrial countries can aid the transition from aid dependency to sustainable development by opening their markets unconditionally to all exports of the poor countries (except arms). This should be a major plank of an international strategy for poverty eradication. The European Union has demonstrated an important gesture, and the rest should follow.

These ideas might sound like dreams. But so did many ideas that have ultimately become the orthodoxy. But the ideas are simple and indeed feasible to implement. What is needed is the political will to act. Development finance is waiting to be rediscovered in the Post-Cold War era of intense globalization. Ultimately, no tinkering at the margin will work. Over time, we see a world where the current unsustainable system of borrowing by, and lending to, the poorest countries is replaced by a predictable system of mandatory transfers (grants).

But this will never be a substitute for strong national commitment to create and sustain prosperity. To translate these ideas into practice requires more than sound economic arguments. It is a political struggle, at the national and international arena. As globalization intensified there has also emerged the internationalization of NGOs: the Jubilee 2000, Oxfam, or the coalition that brought about the Seattle and Prague fiascos. These groups are forcing people to think and, we hope, ultimately, to act to change the world in more fundamental ways.

Notes

1. For Sub-Saharan Africa, the stock of external debt is about 70 percent of GDP, and ~~gulps~~ swallows about 20-30 percent of annual export proceeds in service payments. Nigeria's total debt stock is still contentious, because of poor debt recording and management prior to the setting up of the Debt Management Office (DMO). Pending the outcome of an ongoing reconciliation exercise, the DMO puts the tentative total stock at about US$28 billion (67 percent of gross domestic product (GDP)), although some independent estimates put the figure at about US32 to 35 billion. Out of this DMO figure, unpaid arrears on principal and interest, including penalties for late interest payment amount to about US$20 billion (71 percent). Debt to the Paris Club is about 70 percent of the stock. Note however that excluding the arrears, the balance on what Nigeria borrowed is only about US$8 billion. So far, Nigeria borrowed about US$13 billion, but it has repaid a total of about US$21 billion in service payments, and current projections of debt service payments, 2001-2020 (after rescheduling and without new commitments) is about US$43 billion. Thus, by 2020, Nigeria ~~would~~ will have paid about US$64 billion in debt service for the US$13 billion it borrowed or five times the amount borrowed (US$5 dollars for every 1 dollar borrowed).
2. Several volumes have been written on the tragic state of Africa as the world's lingering development puzzle, and we ~~don't~~ do not intend to rehearse the features of

that tragedy here. The recent collaborative work by the World Bank and four pan African institutions— UN Economic Commission for Africa, ECA, African Economic Research Consortium, AERC, African Development Bank, AfDB, and Global Coalition for Africa (GCA) (see World Bank et al., 2000d 2000)— contains a useful catalogue of the problems. Also, see the World Bank (2000b) *World Development Report, 2000/2001—Attacking Poverty*—for a detailed treatment of the extent and pervasiveness of poverty and inequality.

3. There is a huge literature on why past development finance failed to deliver development. Beside the recipient countries' own weak institutional and governance systems as well as other features which that circumscribed aid effectiveness, there is a growing consensus that much of the lending/aid was not delivered to effect development. The delivery mechanism was faulty, and in many cases money was given to trusted allies rather than to development partners. Also, lending/aid was made to buy reforms, but evidence has also shown that it does not work. So, there is a sense of shared responsibility but unfortunately, the debtors are meant to bear a disproportionate burden of the adjustment.

4. Other papers in this conference focus on the evaluation of the alternative debt relief proposals and the options available to Nigeria. I do not rehearse the evaluation here. But suffice it to note that these initiatives—for debt relief and poverty reduction—represent important first steps forward. Many analysts believe that the world economy and the creditors are

capable of doing much more.

5. Many people, however, question the basis for, or the realism of, such targets that seem largely dead on arrival. ManyPeople also question the consistency between the short-run economic policy instrument—annual budgets—and the policy goals in these documents. For example, government spending that amounts to about 70 percent of non oil GDP that squeezes out the private sector through high interest rates, volatile and depreciating currency, and galloping prices—is hardly the best way to promote private sector—led approach to poverty eradication and growth.

6. Some analysts worry that rooting for outright debt cancellation might affect the perceptions of credit worthiness of the country, and hence hurt its ability to access the international financial market in the near future. That argument is tenuous. First, the ultimate and most important determinant of the country's risk rating is the state of the economy. If Nigeria gets outright cancellation, and also signals to the world that it can now effectively take charge of its resource management and economy, then private finance would flow in. Foreign direct investment, which is what Nigeria really wants rather than government borrowing, flows to the most profitable and secure locations. Conversely, Nigeria cannot hope to be 'credible' and garner low risk rating by living with the debt burden and a comatose economy. Empirical evidence shows that the mere presence of the debt on the books attract high risk premium. Furthermore, Nigeria has never been heavily dependent on foreign borrowing, and its net resource transfers to the rest of the world has been negative. So,

there is, in effect, no extra benefit from letting the debt hang on its neck.
7. *The World Development Report, 2000* (World Bank (2000b)p. vi), argues that a global action is required both to ensure that the opportunities from global integration and technological advance benefit poor people and to manage the risks of insecurity and exclusion that may result from global change. Consequently, it recommends five key actions: (a) promoting global financial stability and opening the markets of rich countries to the agricultural goods, manufactures, and services of poor countries; (b) bridging the digital and knowledge divides, thus bringing technology and information to people throughout the world; (c) providing financial and nonfinancial resources for international public goods, especially medical and agricultural research; (d) increasing aid and debt relief to help countries take actions to end poverty, within a comprehensive framework that puts countries themselves—not external aid agencies—at the center of the design of development strategy; and (e) giving a voice to poor countries and poor people in global forums, including through international links with organizations of poor people.
8. Sachs (2000b) observes that at the core of the global divide is the vast inequality in innovation and diffusion of technology. World Bank lending and grants for science and technology are probably less each year than one tenth of the research and development (R&D) budget of a single large American U.S. pharmaceutical company. For example, the World Bank devotes around US$50 million a year to tropical agri-

cultural research, around US$10 million to tropical health research, and a little more in a scattering of other loans. Merck's research and development R&D budget in 1999 was US$2.1 billion.
9. If basic capability—education, health, and nutrition—is very central to productivity at the national level, it is even more so for the global economy. Empirical estimates are needed of the potential impact of productivity improvements of the world's poorest populations on global output/income.
10. The U.K. Home Office estimates that about 30 million people are smuggled across international borders every year, and that the trade is worth between US$12 to US$20 billion. Illegal immigration rate from China into Britain is estimated at more than 600 a month, and most are being smuggled in container lorries (*The Economist*, June 24, 2000, p.47).
11. Ideas about the nature of the global governance structure required are still evolving. While many analysts agree that the current system is inappropriate or inadequate (see the U.S. bipartisan Meltzer Report on reforming the Bretton Woods institutions), there is no consensus about the particular structure. For example, suggestions usually polarize into two extremes:— those who want more centralized governance structure (world federal government?) with mandatory powers to take care of the disadvantaged, and those who favor some "modifications or strengthening" of the existing institutions. Needless to say that there are those who are happy with the current state of things. A new multilateral coordination would also ensure safety of lives and property all over the world, and also

make everywhere safe and profitable for investment. It would require new global and regional security arrangements.
12. Sachs (2000) argues, for example, that the technological leader and beacon of hope for much of the world, the United States has been the meanest donor of all. It musters a trifling US5 per American each year in budget assistance for the poorest countries. Indeed, except three countries, all the OECD countries have consistently failed to meet the international aid budget since the 1990s.
13. For example, just imagine what a globalization tax of just 1 percent of GDP of the richest countries can provide—probably more than US200,000 billion per annum.

References

Agenor, P. R., and Montiel, P. 1999. *Development Macroeconomics*, 2nd ed. Princeton University Press.

Bethelmy, J. C., 2001. *Emerging Africa*. Development Center Studies, OECD, Paris.

Castells, Manuel. 1998. *The Information Age: Economy, Society and Culture*. Vol. III: *End of A Millennium*. Oxford: Blackwell.

Center for International Development. 1999. *Implementing Debt Relief for the HIPCs*. Cambridge, Mass.: Harvard University.

Chhibber, A., and S. Pahwa. 1993. "Investment Recovery and Growth in Nigeria: The Case for Debt-Relief." Research Report. World Bank, Washington, D.C.

O'Connell, S., and C. C. Soludo, 2001. "Aid Intensity in Africa." *World Development* Vol. 29, No, 9, pp. 1527–52.

Sachs, J. D. 2000a. "A New Global Consensus on Helping the Poorest of the Poor." Paper presented at the 2000 Annual World Bank Conference on Development Economics.

Sachs, J. D., 2000b. "Sachs on Globalization: A New Map of the World." *The Economist.* June 24: 99–101.

Sahn, D. 1992. "Public Expenditures in Sub-Saharan Africa During a Period of Economic Reforms." *World Development* 20(5): 673–93.

Soludo, C. C. 2000a. "Globalization Tax and Trade as Remedies to Underdevelopment Traps and Ineffective Aid." Paper presented at the 12th World Bank Annual Conference on Development Economics, Washington, D.C.

Soludo, C. C. 2000b. "Disputing the Castellian Globalization for Africa." In J. Muller, N. Cloete and S. Badat, eds., *Challenges of Globalization: South Africa Debates with Manuel Castells.* Cape Town, Maskew Miller Longman.

UNDP 1999. *Human Development Report 1999.* New York: Oxford University Press.

World Bank 1996. *Poverty Reduction and the World Bank: Progress and Challenges in the 1990s.* Washington, D.C.

_____.1999. "Building Poverty Reduction Strategies in Developing Countries." Processed. Washington, D.C.

_____. 2000b. *World Development Report, 2000/2001: Attacking Poverty.* New York: Oxford University Press.

_____. 2000d. *Can Africa Claim the 21st Century?* Report. Washington, D.C.: The World Bank

Box 3: Debt Relief: A Fresh Start That Also Serves Donors' Interests

This is a quote from Lawrence Summers, Secretary of the Treasury under President Bill Clinton as reported in *The Washington Post* (1999):

There is a new and innovative approach to reducing poverty through debt reduction in the world's poorest countries. This initiative has attracted a unique global coalition of political and religious leaders, including representatives of both major parties in the United States, grass-roots organizations around the world, and the Vatican. Writing down debts that will never be repaid reflects economic logic. It is also a moral imperative for the world's richest economy. But it is equally a national strategic imperative that as we respond to problems around the world we respond with equal vigor in Africa, where more people have died in conflicts in this decade than in all other regions combined.

When we help these countries build the basis for growth and stability, we help prevent future crisis—and so provide important forward defense of our interests. Building a safer world for Americans out of the ashes of the Cold War has reduced our annual defense budget by US$107 billion in real terms in the past 10 years. President Clinton's proposal would re-invest less than US$1 billion in four years towards supporting the global initiative in debt reduction. This would serve the United States' core interests in several areas.

First, it would provide the right kind of finance for these economies. Private banks write down claims that can no longer be repaid, because keeping sterile loans on the books serves nobody's interests. The alternative is to lend the borrowers more money simply in order to service previous loans. A cynical cycle of this kind of defensive lending discourages private investment, rewards free-riding creditors and does little to promote economic development. Second, it establishes a principle of national responsibility for economic performance. If we have learned anything from the history of economic development, it is that national governments shape national outcomes.

Saddled by a mountain of unpayable debt, governments have a ready excuse for poor performance. Clearing away that debt in return for strong policy makes it easier for people to hold their leaders accountable for economic outcomes—and greatly strengthens the incentive to implement long overdue reforms.

We saw in Poland and Egypt that debt relief, which won strong bipartisan support here in the United States, could provide vital early momentum to reformers and help countries put decades of economic failure behind them. With the Enhanced HIPC we have a chance of seeing this happen in Africa.

Third, this initiative will support more people-centered policies in places where children are today more likely to die before reaching the age of five than to learn to read, and corruption and poor governance are major blocks to economic growth.

With the new framework in place, countries would not receive further debt relief without demonstrating their commitment to strong policies aimed at rapid growth and poverty reduction. Nor would they receive relief without credible ways of demonstrating that savings produced by reduced debt servicing obligations will result in higher levels of spending on reducing infant mortality and other core social goals.

Fourth, and supporting this objective, it establishes a new framework for providing international assistance to these countries—one that moves beyond a closed, IMF-centered process that has too often focused on narrow macroeconomic objectives at the expense of broader human development. In its place would be a new, more open and inclusive process that would involve multiple international organizations and give national policy makers and civil society groups a more central role.

Fifth, it maximizes our financial effectiveness in promoting the right kind of change in these economies. Because of the leverage implicit in our own contribution, and the contribution from other countries that our support would set in train, every dollar we appropriate for this effort could leverage as much as US$90 in debt relief for these economies.

The future of this global effort is in our hands. The rest of the world will not move forward without us. If we fail to play our part, we will stall a major international initiative—and raise yet another question mark about the genuineness of the United States' commitment to a more prosperous and stable world.

In the end, the only ones who can offer the poorest countries a better future are their own governments and citizens. But we can serve America's deepest interests, and those of the global economy as a whole, by helping these countries make a fresh start.

Source: *The Washington Post* (1999, p. A35).

3
Sustainable Debt and Development Strategy in Africa

CYRIL ENWEZE
Vice President, African Development Bank

The Challenge of Debt

It is something of an irony that, looking back, we might regard the 1960s as Africa's Golden Years, at least in light of the optimism that greeted the emergence of many African countries into independence. By the 1970s and the 1980s, heavy reliance on foreign financing, especially bilateral and multilateral loans contributed to the rapid buildup of the continent's external debt. For many of these countries the external debt burden has reached unsustainable levels; large foreign debt and high interest rates, combined with adverse terms of trade, as well as poor macroeconomic policies, have rendered debt service payments simply unmanageable. It is therefore not surprising that no fewer than 33 African countries are now classified as a Heavily Indebted Poor

Country (HIPC).

Africa's stock of external debt currently stands at an estimated US$333.3 billion. The advent of the debt crisis in the early 1980s resulted in a sudden and drastic reduction in the scale of voluntary lending to particularly heavily indebted developing economies. This was a reflection of a sharp reversal in the perceived ability of the public sectors in these countries to service their debts on market terms. Many indebted developing nations experienced a decline in economic growth, investment, and domestic savings. Poor governance and the resultant increase in capital flight from the region have exacerbated the detrimental effects on investment and growth of the debt overhang. For Africa as a whole the investment rate in the 1990s averaged about 16.8 percent of gross domestic product (GDP) compared to 23.2 percent in the 1970s. The decline was even more severe in the lower income African countries.

In addition, Africa's debt problem has a domestic dimension that has also become problematic. Domestic debt has been increasing rapidly in Africa, growing at 8 percent annually during 1985 to 89 and at about 20 percent in the 1990s. It now constitutes a substantial percentage of the GDP. Excessive government domestic borrowing can have a number of adverse effects, including significant reduction of the scope of government spending on social and economic infrastructure and a reduction of the amount the private sector can borrow or the capital it can raise in the market, thus crowding out private investments. Excessive borrowing can also significantly increase interest rates, thus deterring investments, as cost of capital becomes more expensive.

Furthermore, deficit financing by borrowing from the Central Bank, through money creation, fuels inflation, depreciates the exchange rates, and puts pressures on the exchange reserves position. The building up of huge debts today means heavy debt servicing payments in the future, which implies high taxation for future generations. Excessive domestic debt affects a country's credit rating and therefore the cost of its borrowing. Finally, domestic debt can accumulate to levels where they become unsustainable, precipitating all economic crisis where the government defaults to its own residents, culminating in a banking crisis.

The Challenge of Development

The difficulty of external and domestic debt service, while simultaneously financing development and poverty reduction, constitutes a major challenge to African countries. The dynamic dimensions of the challenge are linked to:

- Past inability to implement institutional reforms and prudent macroeconomic management for sustained periods
- Problems of governance, which lead to misallocation of resources and a lack of transparency in public affairs, preventing the creation and maintenance of a climate conducive to the development of the private sector and to investment, including foreign investment, thereby retarding growth
- Weak institutional, administrative, and technical

capacities, hindering the preparation and implementation of appropriate policies and strategies
- Weakness of democratic institutions and the resurgence of civil disturbance and armed conflict, which impede the effective and sustained implementation of economic policies and social development; and the wider implications of conflict on the countries in and out of conflict, and on the neighboring countries
- Major endemic diseases, such as HIV/AIDS and malaria, which result in high mortality rates and place a heavy burden on the continent's future.

Overall, a generally negative perception of the continent persists, which limits Africa's ability to attract foreign direct investment, and to accelerate economic growth.

The Emergence of Hope

There is a beam of hope. Africa entered the new millennium with some renewed signs of progress and a relatively broad commitment to reform that augur well for the future. For the first time in a generation there are signs of economic progress in Africa. In some countries sound economic reforms have helped to reduce macroeconomic imbalances, to eliminate distortions, and to improve overall economic efficiency.

- Average real growth has exceeded 3 percent in the last five years, or more than three times the average for the preceding five years

- Real per capita incomes have also risen in many countries since the mid-1990s
- Rates of inflation have fallen sharply in several countries, reducing the continent's average from close to 30 percent at the beginning of the 1990s to about 13 percent last year.

The story is not just one of better economic indicators. Increasingly, in many countries attention is also being given to achieving high quality growth, as reform efforts have focused on reducing poverty by placing higher priority on public spending on health care, education, and other basic social services. Infant mortality, life expectancy, and adult literacy have been improving over the last decade. Moreover, many African countries have made some progress in freeing the private sector from cumbersome government controls on prices, international trade, investments, and foreign exchange.

For some countries implementation of these economic policies has been accompanied by political liberalization and a shift toward participatory forms of government that foster consensus in policy making. Checks and balances are also being strengthened along with peaceful changeovers of political power.

Improving Africa's Development Prospects

Recent achievements have been encouraging, but they are not enough to make a dent in the pervasive poverty picture of the continent. It is now generally acknowledged that Africa needs sustainable growth rates of approximately 8 to 10 percent to fight poverty effectively. It is indeed feasible to achieve such growth rates. The continent has the potential. While the international community should assist, we must realize, however, that ultimately Africa holds its destiny in its own hands.

The Role of African Countries

African countries must take the initiative in maintaining and intensifying the virtuous circle of better policies and higher growth. Lessons of development in Africa and elsewhere learned over the years indicate that the focus should be on at least five key policy areas:

- Enhancing good governance, which will increase the prospects of success. We failed to develop in the past because we did not give adequate attention to the importance of having predictable regulatory frameworks and transparent public administrations as well as functional judiciary systems. We also failed to ensure good governance in the utilization of resources, thereby contributing to the creation of the debt overhang problem. Good governance requires robust and publicly accountable institutions to formulate and implement policies, promote transparency, and fight corruption. It also involves fostering a participatory reform process, both in terms of giving civil society a voice in decision making as well as the means, through fiscal decentralization, to participate in

the development effort.
- Strengthening macroeconomic policy by reducing fiscal deficits and stabilizing the financial system will help to transform the environment for development. In addition, improving public finance management by paying particular attention to public expenditures, even as efforts are made to raise revenues, will also help to contain the growth of both domestic and external debt. Governments should focus on improving the legal, physical, and social infrastructure as well as the institutional development that are necessary prerequisites for rapid growth and effective poverty reduction. Besides, the growth of fiscal deficits absorbs vital savings, fuels the debt problem, and crowds out private investment.
- Creating an enabling environment for investment by avoiding conflicts and civil strife, and by promoting good governance. It is vital to remove the sense of uncertainty that too often plagues investor decision making. African countries should implement policies to benefit from the growth and enhanced role of the private sector in financing development. In addition, the financial sector should be strengthened to enhance financial intermediation and facilitate private investors' access to financing.
- Strengthening human capital development by giving priority to education and health in public expenditure. This is vital not only to spur growth but also to respond to the consequences of poverty.

• Speeding up economic integration by further liberalizing the trade and exchanges that deepen regional integration. This will enable African countries to benefit from growth of foreign direct investments, allow African businesses to expand their sources of financing, and help expand the possibilities for trade. It will also help to boost the efficiency and competitiveness of domestic producers, allow African countries to better overcome the disadvantages of their relatively small economies, and enhance their ability to trade on a global basis while helping them realize economies of scale.

The Role of the International Community

The international community needs to help Africa overcome some of its development challenges. With a compounding debt problem, African countries continue to knock hard on the doors to the markets of developed economies to gain access. Moreover, the image of a resurgent Africa is being undercut by an image of an Africa devastated by HIV/AIDS and malaria, of one mired in political turmoil and armed conflict. With slight variations among individual countries four common critical areas of need have been identified:

- Reduction in the massive debt burden
- Improved access to trade and capital markets of the developed countries
- Addressing the plague of HIV/AIDS and

Malaria
- Assistance via peacekeeping operations in conflict situations.

The international community should continue to provide assistance to regional member countries (RMCs) to reduce their external debt through market based mechanisms.

Admittedly, the international donor community has recently taken a major step to strengthen earlier efforts to reduce the debt of HIPC. The enhanced HIPC framework, in which the African Development Bank (AfDB) participates, does indeed represent a major breakthrough. It is important to note, however, that its success will depend on sufficient resources being made available by the international donor community. This must be backed by a strong credit policy, which ties debt forgiveness and new loans and credits to good fiscal, monetary, and trade policies. In addition, tackling the debt problem of Africa in a comprehensive manner will require the resumption of earlier efforts to address the debt problem of post conflict countries that are, at present, not covered under HIPC.

The donor community also needs to assist African countries in expanding their trade through the full implementation of existing trade arrangements, and expansion of the coverage of such arrangements to other countries. Currently, tariff and nontariff barriers often constrain the growth of African exports. It is essential that the international community take steps to remove such barriers and open their domestic markets to African exports. In this regard, the recent improvements in market access granted by the European Union (for the 48 least developed countries, two thirds of which are African) and by the U.S. government through the Africa Growth Opportunities Act are welcome. However, these improvements must be complemented by efforts to eliminate the huge OECD subsidies (they are currently estimated to equal Africa's entire GDP) that are in and of themselves major constraints to Africa's competitiveness, given the trading relationships between Africa and the OECD countries.

International support for the low-income countries in Africa especially should also consist of increasing the volume of concessional resources by reversing the unfortunate decline in official development assistance (ODA) of recent years. This now stands at 0.22 percent of gross national product (GNP), considerably lower than the goal of 0.7 percent set by the United Nations. About five years ago the international community adopted the International Development Goals (IDG) with the objective of helping to reduce poverty by half by 2015, while also putting developing countries on a sustainable development path. Implementation of the agenda requires substantial resources on the part of the developing countries in addition to resources needed for the implementation of appropriate policies. OECD partners, therefore, need to reconsider their assistance to low-income countries to meet the critical shortfalls in resources.

The international community needs to consolidate their efforts for HIV/AIDS and malaria through collaborative research and ODA assistance targeted at the vulnerable groups of society. Budgetary assistance to community driven programs and locally based nongovernmental organizations NGOs has more immediate impact in the short term. In the long term there is the need to assist RMCs in building their capacity to extend assistance programs to national coverage.Regional Member Countries (RMCs) need the assistance of the international community with societal and ethnic strife especially in peacekeeping operations during, as well as after, conflict situations. Focusing on post-conflict investment may be too late and generally too costly. In addition, where strong bilateral ties exist, these should be relied on for prevention of conflict and social strife.

The Role of the African Development Bank

The AfDB is aware of the constraints and challenges to African development efforts, and we are encouraged that, in spite of these constraints, many African countries are forging ahead with economic and political reforms. The AfDB will continue to lend its support to these efforts. In line with this goal, the AfDB has recently formulated its vision statement to guide its work to focus on those areas critical to Africa's development efforts in poverty reduction. These areas include agriculture and rural development, human resource development, and private sector development at the country level; governance; economic integration and cooperation at the regional level; and environment and gender, which permeate all aspects of the development effort.

Accordingly, considerable efforts were made in the past year to ensure that the various policies of the AfDB, as well as its lending and technical assistance operations, conform to the broad lines and priorities set out in the vision statement. The Bank is continuing to intensify its efforts to increase the level of resources available to its member countries.

The AfDB is a major player in the HIPC initiative, which is attempting to reduce, to a sustainable level, the stock of debt of these countries. Indeed, the AfDB has been involved in the initiative since its inception in 1996, and delivered debt relief amounting to US$141.7 million to Mozambique and Uganda, which reached their completion points in 1998–99. Of this, the AfDB financed US$57.3 from its internal resources. Thus, not only is the AfDB committing its own resources to this cause, it is also mobilizing resources from bilateral development partners.

Following a consultative review of the implementation of the HIPCs initiative in 1998–99, an enhanced framework was introduced to provide for:

- More debt relief to a greater number of countries through reduction in the debt sustainability targets
- Faster debt relief through the introduction of flexibility in the qualifying period and the front-loading of debt relief
- Retroactivity, through the application of the enhanced framework targets to countries that have already qualified for HIPC assistance under the original framework
- Closer linkage between debt relief and poverty reduction through the implementation and monitoring of poverty reduction projects within the context of Poverty Reduction Strategy Papers (PRSPs), prepared by the beneficiary countries

These enhancements have increased the number of eligible African countries from 25 to 31, while the total costs reached US$28.6 billion in 1999 NPV terms, out of which the AfDB will help to finance US$2.3 billion.

Under the enhanced HIPC framework, the modality approved for the AfDB delivery of debt relief to eligible countries has the following features:

- Delivery of debt relief through annual debt service reductions
- Release of up to 80 percent of annual debt service obligations as they come due until the total debt relief is provided
- Interim financing—between the decision and completion points—of up to 40 percent of total debt relief
- Debt service to be provided, whenever possible, within a 15-year time horizon to assist countries in attaining the internationally agreed development goals for the year 2015

Beyond the HIPC debt relief, the AfDB is also pursuing the following initiatives and financing strategies: The AfDB has established an additional debt reduction facility, the Supplementary Financing Mechanism, which provides concessional African Development Fund (ADF) resources to low income (category A) countries to relieve them from the burden of interest payments due on outstanding AfDB debt obligations. The use of ADF resources to cover AfDB obligations will free up member countries' foreign exchange reserves for other uses. These low income countries have access to AfDB resources through the private sector and enclave projects program of the AfDB. Enclave projects refer to those projects in low income countries for which loans are granted on the basis of the project's demonstrated ability to generate sufficient export revenues to meet its loan repayment obligations.

In recognition of the increasing role of the private sector as the engine of growth, the AfDB has upgraded its private sector unit into a full department with larger resources—both financial and human—to enhance its investment capacity. We are also looking at effective instruments such as lines of credit to put more resources at the disposal of the private sector in our RMCs.

The AfDB has adopted a performance-based allocation mechanism in its concessional resources window. Countries that perform on clearly defined objective criteria are rewarded with larger resource allocations.

Finally, the AfDB is playing a catalytic role, mobilizing resources through cofinancing with others, including multilateral and bilateral agencies, and contributing to increased inflows of private capital by assisting countries in creating the enabling environment through policy reforms. The AfDB has intensified collaboration with its development partners, especially the World Bank and the International Monetary Fund (IMF), and is seeking to strengthen collaboration with the European Union, United Nations agencies, and other multilateral and bilateral partners.

In partnership with the World Bank and IMF, AfDB is also playing a major role in the recent initiative to develop PRSPs. It collaborated fully with other international financial institutions in organizing the preparatory workshops and, indeed, hosted the ministerial workshop in Abidjan in March 2000. The AFDB is also responding to requests from the RMCs to assist in preparing their PRSPs.

Conclusion

The AfDB will continue to bolster its efforts to provide effective and quality assistance to its regional member countries toward implementation of policies for sustained development and poverty reduction. It will continue with its main mission of resource mobilization, and in the next few months we will negotiate the ninth replenishment of the ADF. The mid-term review of the ADF-VIII indicated strong support for the direction that the Bank has taken in the last few years and the activities that it finances. We, therefore, expect to mobilize considerable concessional resources to help the Bank fulfill its mission effectively.

The Bank's assistance will only bear fruit in those countries where conditions for sustained economic growth are in place. In a nutshell, the task at hand is to convince markets to increase investments in Africa; and this, in turn, requires the implementation of credible policies, including good governance, on a sustained basis by the African countries. Frankly, it is that succinct. With the movement toward sustained growth being made in some African countries so far, we hope that we can forge effective partnerships to address the challenges.

4

Debt Relief
What Has Been Achieved, What Needs to be Done

CALLISTO MADAVO
Vice President, Africa Region
The World Bank

Africa, the only continent in which the number of poor people is increasing—needs to raise its economic growth to at least 7 percent to reverse this trend. To do that Africa as a whole will need to raise its investment rate to at least 25 percent, for which it will need to rely substantially on foreign savings for finance. Borrowing, and therefore debt, is a legitimate part of everyday economic management. Countries can borrow to finance investments that otherwise would not be possible, thus accelerating growth and the delivery of key services to the community. Of course, an unsustainable buildup of debt creates its own problems, and becomes a disincentive to new investors and crowds out spending for essential services. At the outset, therefore, it is important to underline that debt relief—or debt cancellation—is not an end in itself but, rather, a means to securing resources needed for development.

Calls for debt relief for developing countries have been part of the international scene and the subject of conferences for many years. In the 1980s, when large unpayable debts mostly owed by Latin American countries to commercial banks threatened the functioning of the financial system, the international community responded with debt reduction schemes such as the Baker and Brady plans to address the problem, and was successful. However, low-income countries with debts owed mainly to official creditors were largely left out. Those countries continued to borrow, and in some cases their incomes failed to keep pace with their rising debts. Many of those countries happen to be in Africa. Today, the debt issue has become mainly an African one.

In the mid-1990s the acuteness of the debt problems of low-income countries became inescapably clear. James Wolfensohn, the then new president of the World Bank, put the issue of debt relief on the map, and in 1996 the World Bank along with the International Monetary Fund (IMF), launched the Heavily Indebted Poor Countries (HIPCs) debt relief initiative. After an initial round, the program was significantly enhanced in 1999 so as to provide faster and deeper relief.

Achievements Under HIPC

In the year or so following the approval of the enhanced HIPC in late 1999, we have seen a remarkable delivery of debt relief for poor countries: US$34 billion in debt relief for 22 countries agreed to and being delivered right now. Of these, 18 countries are in Africa, with US$25 billion in relief agreed. To cite a few specifics of what this means for the 22 countries:

- Debts are being reduced by 50 percent from the HIPC initiative, and by two thirds counting complementary action by bilateral creditors
- Annual debt service is now being reduced by about US$1.1 billion per year relative to what was actually being paid in prior years (1998–99). This is freeing up resources equivalent to more than 1 percent of gross domestic product (GDP)
- The burden of annual debt service will fall from 16 percent of exports and 27 percent of revenues prior to HIPC to an estimated 8 percent and 12 percent over the next few years, respectively. This is actually less than the debt service of most of the non HIPC countries
- This relief will enable countries to substantially increase social spending. After debt relief, social spending is expected to increase by US$1.7 billion per year to an average of 7 percent of GDP, compared with 2 percent of GDP that will be due for debt service. This is how debt relief is helping to fund schools, health clinics, rural roads, and campaigns to address HIV/AIDS.

Moreover, complementary debt relief from bilateral creditors will release even more resources and add space for investments to power pro-poor growth in the countries concerned.

Why this remarkable development? First, HIPC relief has flowed from an *internationally agreed framework* (rather than unilateral action on the part of either debtors or individual creditors). A key feature of that framework is that it is built on objective criteria and on principles that balance the interests of creditors and debtors. These principles include:

- Equitable treatment among debtors, based on a common standard (that is, of reducing debts to the equivalent of 150 percent of exports)
- Linkage to good economic management and poverty reduction strategies, so that debt relief is seen as a recognition of current good policy, rather than as a sign of poor management. This is important not only to avoid the moral hazard of creating a reward for mismanagement, but also to ensure that the resources liberated though debt relief will be applied to poverty reduction, and that the foundations will be laid for countries to secure investment and finance in the future
- Equitable treatment among creditors, so that each creditor is expected to provide its proportional share of the relief, based on how much it is owed after traditional relief has been exhausted
- Additionally to ongoing aid programs, so that the resources provided through debt relief can enable an expansion of programs for poverty reduction
- Maintenance of the financial integrity of multilateral institutions, so that they may continue to

be providers of new resources.

This approach acknowledges that both creditors and debtors contributed to the buildup of debt problems, and that it is a collective responsibility to address these problems and their root causes.

Second, the debt has been able to *be financed*. For the World Bank this has been achieved initially by contributions of net income from the International Bank for Reconstruction and Development (IBRD), and then by promises of future reimbursements to the International Development Association (IDA) by donors. This funding is important to ensure that World Bank debt relief—some US$4.8 billion agreed so far—will not reduce its ability to provide new concessional credits. For other multilateral development banks, however, financing has already required significant contributions from donors—some US$2.5 billion so far—to enable them to participate.

Third, this initiative has received broad acceptance, because it is a *cooperative and comprehensive arrangement*, whereby all IDA-only countries are offered a clear path to bring their debt down to an affordable level.

The Challenges Ahead

The HIPC program is not over, and nor is it a complete response. There are three main challenges to going forward. First, to extend decisions under the HIPC framework to more countries that are eligible. This is a major challenge, because many of the HIPCs that have not yet qualified have been in conflict, or have had serious governance problems (countries such as Somalia, the Republic of Congo, Sierra Leone, and Sudan).

We are continuing to innovate, in particular to accommodate the special circumstances of countries that are emerging from conflict. Flexibility will be our watchword for these post-conflict cases, as we seek to help those devastated economies that face, in some cases, accumulated arrears and ruined performance records that might otherwise block their path to standard debt relief. We are working hard to assist those countries whose situations will require a creative approach to measuring performance and dealing with their financial problems.

Second, we need to recognize that the resource requirements of low-income countries extend well beyond debt relief. During the 1990s, the 22 countries that have already qualified for HIPC debt relief were receiving external resources—net of all debt service—that were equivalent to about 10 percent of their GDP to supplement domestic savings in order to finance their development. Most of these resources were in the form of official aid, provided mainly as grants and supplemented by concessional loans.

These resources will continue to be needed, but their availability is uncertain. During the 1990s average gross flows were about US$10 billion per year to the 22 HIPCs that have qualified for debt relief. A reduction by only 10 percent of these flows would offset all that has been mobilized through debt relief. A 20 percent cut would offset even a total cancellation of debt service. Yet, since the early 1990s, aid budgets have been declining as a share of Organization for Economic Cooperation and Development (OECD) GNP. In Sub-Saharan Africa, aid receipts have fallen from US$32 per capita in 1990 to only US$19 by 1998. This underlines again that debt relief can be only part of the solution.

Why has aid fallen? It was often said that budget constraints in donor countries limited the availability of aid. Yet, there has been no increase in aid commensurate with the recent fiscal strengthening in OECD countries. It is now clearer than ever that concerns over aid effectiveness have significantly constrained the availability of aid, just as perceptions of risk and the high cost of doing business in Africa have constrained increases in private investment, both domestic and foreign. There are too few success stories. Africans need to create some—and soon!

Third, and perhaps most important challenge that we are facing; the need to improve the way external and internal resources are used. Unless the root causes of the debt buildup of the past are addressed, including low returns on investment, and a better use of Africa's potential—including the potential of its people—then long-term debt sustainability will not be achieved, and poverty rates will not come down. We need to confront the HIV/AIDS pandemic, which threatens to erode all the development gains so painfully achieved over the past three decades.

Africa's average return on investment, as indicated by the amount of growth that is associated with the rate of investment, has been little more than one half of that in other developing regions. At the same time, dependency on external savings has been far greater, and, unlike the situation in other regions, most of the resources flowing into Africa have been public. Relative to GDP, public resource flows into Africa, excluding North and South Africa, have been more than five times as high as those into South Asia, the other region with very low average income.

There are many reasons for low returns on public investment. Surely, one of them is that public spending decisions have been all too often made in secret without transparency or public accountability. Responsibility for the poor use of external resources in the past lies not only in Africa. The Cold War and commercial pressures also contributed to poor lending decisions. Improved discipline among lenders is, therefore, also part of the challenge for better use of resources.

However, better governance through broad-based participation offers hope for more effective use of public resources. Efforts are being made, in connection with HIPC, to ensure that governments put in place budget and financial management systems that account properly for public spending. These systems are needed not only so that OECD governments can account to their taxpayers for the use of aid, but also as an essential part of building a strong, working democracy, and for ensuring that citizens and parliaments of African countries can know how their own resources are being used.

Accountability to domestic constituencies is at the heart of better use for resources. The grounding of external assistance in poverty reduction strategy papers (PRSPs) that are developed under national leadership with broad public participation offers hope that not only will internal and external resources be used more effectively but that they will do so with an explicit objective of reducing poverty.

Finally, it is important to keep our eyes on *the long-term needs for private resources* to bear the bulk of the resources needs for growth and development. Debt relief is helping, and we see, in cases such as Uganda, that private investors respond well when an unsustainable debt overhang is removed. But this is not automatic. Relief needs to be provided in a way that lays the foundations for a sound investment climate that will attract resources, and provide the incentives for them to be used well.

The Contentious Issue of Debt Cancellation

Some have made calls for total debt cancellation for poor countries, and some have further extended this to include middle-income countries. Many of those calls are well-intentioned. And there is no doubt that the progress that has been made on debt relief would not have happened were it not for the forceful and politically effective contributions to the pressure for debt relief for poor countries that has come from religious organizations and non-governmental organizations.

On the surface, the idea of full debt cancellation for poor countries has a certain appeal. After all, if the HIPC initiative and related relief are resulting in a reduction of the debt by two thirds, why not go all the way? But things are not so simple. This perhaps is the wrong focus and these proposals are seriously flawed for three reasons:

- If limited to the existing group of HIPCs, proposals for full debt cancellation are inequitable among debtors and the world's poor. If the right level of debt is considered to be zero for HIPCs, there is simply no basis to exclude other equally

poor countries such as India or Bangladesh. The number of poor people in Bangladesh, for example, is more than double that of the HIPCs combined.
- Full debt cancellation would cripple or even close the multilateral development system, unless financed by additional contributions from bilateral donors. Regional institutions such as the African Development Bank Group have the largest share of representation on their boards from developing countries, yet these are the most vulnerable. If 100 percent cancellation were extended to all 64 low-income countries, then it would effectively result in the liquidation of the entire multilateral development bank system. For IDA, the write off would be equivalent to more than 80 percent of its entire outstanding claims. Since IDA finances about half of its new commitments from repayments of past loans, this would cut in half IDA's new commitments, about US$6.5 billion per year, unless donors were prepared to double their contributions. This seems highly unlikely. For the IBRD, the write off would be US$29 billion, equivalent to more than 100 percent of its total equity and 18 years of its net income. Indeed, an increase of 1 percentage point in the cost of IBRD borrowing—an event that could easily occur if IBRD's finances were compromised, even if the entire institution were not threatened—could cost its borrowers about US$1 billion per year on existing loans.

- The result would likely be less, not more, net financial flows to the poorest developing countries. The IBRD and IDA alone are providing between US$1.5 and US$2.0 billion per year to low income countries in net transfers, that is after taking into account all debt service. Equally important, the concept and reality that lending and financial intermediation is a fundamental part of the development process would be wrecked, and lending for development—official and private—would dry up. This is not the way to lay the foundations for growth.

In some ways, however, the greatest difficulty with the proposals for total cancellation is that they are diverting attention from the big issue: effective use of the resources available. By this we mean not just current resources, but also the potential *impact* of new resource flows. Aid today from OECD countries is only 0.2 percent of their GNP. If these countries were simply to raise this aid even back to the 0.3 percent of their GNP that it was only 10 or so years ago, it would imply an increase of net official development assistance of some US$25 billion per year.

What does this mean for Nigeria?

Nigeria is in an unusual situation. It is a low-income country, with current income levels below even the average for Sub-Saharan Africa. In dollar terms, income levels have fallen by some 40 percent in the last quarter century, despite its enormous energy and fiscal resources. Debt is a part of the problem—an important part—but it differs in a number of ways from that of other low-income countries, and there will need to be a different way to deal with it.

First, more than three-quarters of Nigeria's debt of $32 billion at the end of last year was owed to bilateral Paris Club creditors, and less than 12 percent was owed to multilateral creditors. Most of this debt was contracted on commercial or nonconcessional terms.

Second, even though Nigeria has a significant debt burden, that burden is, in some respects, not as heavy in relation to its resources, especially oil. By one measure Nigeria's US$32 billion in debt is equivalent to a little more than 200 percent of its exports of goods and nonfactor services in today's dollars. Before HIPC relief, the 22 countries that are receiving debt relief had all average debt to export ratio of 260 percent, which is being brought down under the HIPC initiative to less than 150 percent. Another way of looking at it is that debt service for Nigeria in 2001 appears likely to be equivalent to about 12 percent of export revenues, compared with about 17 percent for other HIPCs before relief

Third, though Nigeria's debt (before any debt relief) was almost 40 percent above the HIPC debt sustainability threshold at the end of last year, it could reach that level within a year or so, barring a collapse of the oil price or a significant adverse movement of the dollar. Thus, debt sustainability may be in sight whether through more debt relief or growth in exports and revenues. Nevertheless, small changes in the oil price can have significant impact.

The Way Forward

The Paris Club rescheduling, which reduced the debt service due in 2001 from US$5.3 billion to US$3.2 billion, was a good start on regularizing the position with external creditors and markets. But what Nigeria really needs is a Paris Club "Plus," where the "plus" refers to addressing the overhang of debt, and if necessary by further restructuring and perhaps bringing relief to Nigerian debt securely to a sustainable level. It also means complementing debt relief with new resources on appropriate terms, and reforming the economy so that it can diversify away from oil dependency.

It also means strengthening the institutions and processes that would prevent unproductive borrowing in the future; that is, stronger debt and macroeconomic management, but also transparency and accountability to the public so that borrowing is done with public consciousness of its implications.

Most important, it means keeping attention focused on the way resources are used. The 10 percent of oil revenues being spent on debt service is a cost. But the future rests even more on how well the other 90 percent of Nigeria's revenues are employed. Relative to the past, there is room for a great deal of gain in this area. Ordinary Nigerians have not seen much benefit from public spending in the past, and progress is essential if they are to perceive a "democracy dividend." Public vigilance over budgetary allocations and monitoring of outcomes is a path to better decisions and delivery of services.

That is why the PRSP process is so important to Nigeria now. By involving the population in the preparation of the government's development strategy, keeping poverty reduction as the central objective of that strategy, preparation of the PRSP can be vital in helping Nigeria in democratizing its development process. The democratization of Nigeria's development may be the most important—and lasting—component of its democracy dividend.

A Paris Club Plus, devised seamlessly with that PRSP process, would give Nigeria's external partners an unprecedented opportunity to help consolidate that democracy dividend, first by providing resources responsibly and, second, by opening up markets so as to enhance Nigeria's own export earning potential to enable diversification away from oil to foster pro-poor growth. Nigeria has a great deal of potential in the nonoil sectors, including agriculture. With the correct policies and open markets in the industrial countries, Nigeria could develop many other sources of income in addition to oil and gas.

Nigeria's future is not only for Nigeria. The hopes of much of Africa reside in the achievements of one of its potential powerhouses. Resolving the debt issue is one element—one critical element—of the solution. However, Nigeria needs a solution that goes beyond the debt issue. It needs a Paris Club Plus. Debt relief will not bear fruit if Nigeria's other, more important development issues, are not addressed effectively.

5
External Debt, Capital Flight, and Growth in Nigeria

S. IBI AJAYI
Professor of Economics
University of Ibadan, Ibadan, Nigeria

T he external debt crisis of Sub-Saharan Africa, like its Latin American counterpart, is not yet over. A significant number of countries in Sub-Saharan Africa have, in general, adopted a development strategy that relies heavily on foreign financing from both official and private sources. This, unfortunately, has meant that for many countries in the region the stock of external debt has built up over recent decades to a level that is widely viewed as unsustainable (Ajayi and Khan 2000). This has given rise to concerns about its deleterious effects on investment and growth, principally the well-known "debt overhang" effect. Just as the external indebtedness of Sub-

Saharan African countries worsened in the late 1970s in some cases, and early 1980s in the case of others, capital flight also became a problem.

Thus, Sub-Saharan Africa was both an importer and exporter of capital. In the case of the severely indebted low-income countries, the external debt burden, if anything, has in most cases worsened. Debt indicators show that the overall external debt has become so large relative to the economic size of these countries and relative to export earnings that off setting parts of it in the short term would amount to an impossible burden on those nations (Hope 1996).

The external indebtedness of African countries is becoming more acute for a number of reasons (Ajayi and Khan 2000). First, the external debt is enormous relative to the size of the economy and has led, in many cases, to capital flight and the discouragement of investment, especially private investment. Second, debt servicing payments absorb a major proportion of export earnings and eat significantly into the funds that could be used to provide essential facilities to improve the welfare of a country's citizens. Third, debt burden threatens not only the execution but also the prospects of success of adjustment programs. Fourth, given the time spent on external debt negotiations and its management, debt has a negative impact on an economy's overall growth and growth prospects.

Nigeria is one of the severely indebted low-income countries that is greatly afflicted by heavy external indebtedness, its acknowledged oil wealth notwithstanding. Past efforts at finding solutions to external indebtedness have no doubt been imaginative and generous, but, to the extent that the debt problem lingers or has worsened, these efforts can be adjudged as having been inadequate. As external indebtedness increased so has capital flight. The magnitude of capital flight from developing countries indicates a serious breakdown in domestic policies. Cline (1985) claims that it is largely within the power of debtor countries to limit capital flight by adopting appropriate domestic policies on interest rates, the exchange rates, capital account convertibility, and fiscal balance. Countries with a large debt overhang have been known to run into debt servicing difficulties if the private sector is exporting capital (Charrette 1991). It has been argued that the sources of financial flows for growth in the developing world lie in foreign direct investment and the reversal of capital flight.

In Africa, both of these (that is foreign direct investment and capital flight) have been affected by political instability and unfavorable macroeconomic environment. Given the size of the external indebtedness and capital flight that has taken place over the years, these inevitably have deleterious effects on the economy.

External Debt and Capital Flight in Nigeria

How much does Nigeria owe? There is a general belief among Nigerians that Nigeria does not know exactly how much it owes. Put in a different way, there are arguments about the authenticity of some of the external debts that Nigeria supposedly owed. It was in recognition of the prevailing doubts that in the late 1980s, Nigeria appointed outside consultants to reconcile her external indebtedness. Official figures from the ministry of finance are invariably different from data published by the International Monetary Fund (IMF)/World Bank.

Although Nigeria started borrowing externally in the 1970s, its external indebtedness in that period was relatively small. By 1976 Nigeria's external indebtedness took its upward turn, rising from about US$1.3 billion in 1976 to US$3.2 billion in 1977, a rise of about 146 percent in a single year. The external indebtedness rose thereafter, in single and double digits until it reached a peak of about US$34.0 billion in 1994, and stood at US$30.3 billion in 1998. In constant terms as defined under the table, external debt rose from about US$4 billion in 1971 and reached a peak of about US$36 billion in 1994 tapering off to about US$30 billion in 1997. (See Table 1).

Table 1: Nigeria's External Debt, 1973 - 97

Year	In Current Dollars		In Constant Dollars	
	Debt US$billion	Change (%)	Debt Constant Value[a] (US$b)	Change (%)
1973	1.7	70.0	5.12	37.7
1974	1.8	5.9	3.85	-24.7
1975	1.7	-5.6	3.33	-13.5
1976	1.3	-23.5	2.52	-24.4
1977	3.2	146.2	5.68	125.6
1978	5.1	59.4	8.31	46.1
1979	6.2	21.6	8.52	2.5
1980	8.9	43.5	10.00	17.4
1981	11.4	28.1	12.93	29.3
1982	12.0	5.3	14.32	10.8
1984	17.3	1.1	22.65	3.5
1985	18.6	4.5	24.19	6.8
1986	22.2	19.4	28.10	16.2
1987	29.0	30.6	33.60	19.6
1988	29.6	2.1	34.06	1.4
1989	30.1	1.7	34.17	0.3
1990	33.4	11.0	35.08	2.7
1991	33.5	0.3	35.68	1.7
1992	29.0	-13.4	30.66	-14.1
1993	30.7	5.9	34.49	12.5
1994	33.1	7.8	36.17	4.9
1995	34.0	2.7	34.00	-0.0
1996	31.4	-7.6	31.53	-7.3
1997	28.4	-9.6	29.74	-5.7

[a] calculated as the current value of external debt deflated by the World Unit Import Value Index 1995=100 (Dornbusch and Helmers, 1988).

Source: World Bank, *Global Development Finance, 2000.*

The pattern of external debt in constant terms is not too dissimilar from the current values in terms of its trend and changes, apart from the fact that while external debt in nominal terms rose by about 146 percent between 1976 and 1977, and it rose by about 125 percent in constant terms for the same period.

Chart 1: Nigeria's External Debt, 1971-97 ($Billions)

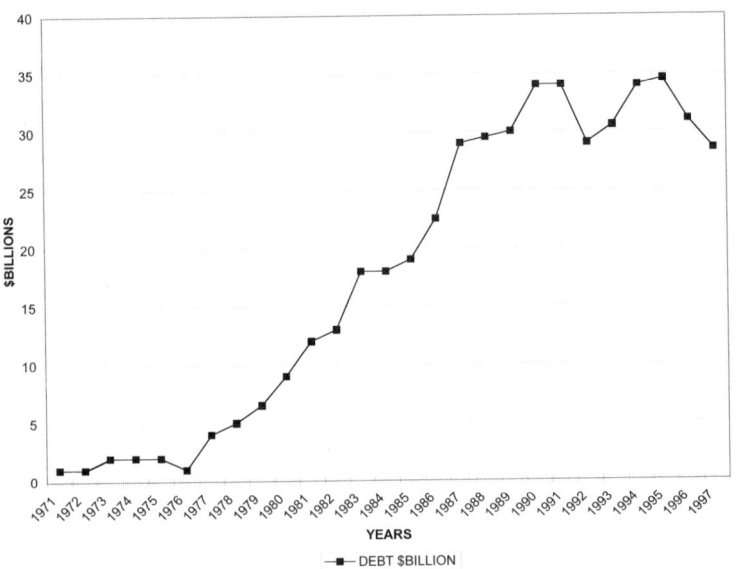

Short-term debt as a percentage of total debt was about 32 percent between 1971 and 1976, but rose briefly to about 69 percent in 1977. After a drop to about 21 percent in 1982, it rose again before the rate dropped steadily in the periods between 1987 and 1991. By 1997, short-term debt stood at about 19 percent of total debt. Multilateral debt's share in total debt varied between 17 percent and 30 percent between 1970 and 1976, and virtually declined steadily thereafter, and stayed steady at 14 percent from 1992. The average interest rate on external debt varied between 4 percent and 11 percent in the period 1971 to 1994.

Table 2: Debt, Its Distribution and Cost, 1971–1997

YEAR	TOTAL STOCK (US$b)	SHORT-TERM DEBT TO TOTAL DEBT (%)	MULTILATERAL DEBT TO TOTAL DEBT (%)	AVERAGE INTEREST (%)
1971	1.0	32.2	22.5	4.5
1972	1.0	32.3	26.1	6.1
1973	1.7	32.3	17.0	6.6
1974	1.8	32.3	17.8	4.5
1975	1.7	32.2	21.6	7.6
1076	1.3	32.3	30.4	8.5
1977	3.2	68.7	14.3	8.2
1978	5.1	48.1	9.6	10.2
1979	6.2	36.6	8.4	10.6
1980	8.9	39.8	6.4	10.5
1981	11.4	38.8	5.5	11.2
1982	12.0	21.0	6.2	9.8
1983	17.6	28.8	5.0	10.2
1984	17.8	32.3	5.4	9.8
1985	18.6	26.8	7.7	8.5
1986	22.2	16.6	10.1	8.6
1987	29.0	5.4	10.6	8.4
1988	29.6	5.2	9.6	7.6
1989	30.1	1.5	10.5	7.0
1990	33.4	4.5	11.2	6.5
1991	33.5	2.6	12.0	6.1
1992	29.0	7.6	14.1	4.6
1993	30.7	12.9	14.1	3.7
1994	33.1	14.6	14.5	7.7
1995	34.0	16.6	14.5	0.0
1996	31.4	18.1	14.3	0.0
1997	28.4	19.4	14.1	0.0

Source: World Bank, *Global Development Finance*, 2000.

According to the data supplied by the Debt Management Office, Nigeria's total external debt as at March 2001 with its composition is shown in table 3. As can be seen from the table, Nigeria's external debt stood at about US$29 billion in March 2001. Of this amount, about 47 percent is owed to Paris Club while 13 percent is owed to the short-term private Paris Club.

Table 3: External Debt, March 31, 2001 (US$ Thousands)

Description	Total
Paris Club (1 to 3) – Public	13,687,131
Paris Club (1 to 3) – Short Term Private	3,848,007
Non-Previously Rescheduled Bilateral	2,913,112
Post Cut off debts due to Paris Club Members	707,543
Sub Total	21,155,794
Less Lump sum Payment	(1,100,420)
Non Paris Club countries — Bilateral	758,297
Non Paris Club countries — Commercial	1,583,629
Sub Total	2,321,926
Less Lump sum Payment	(49,250)
Multilateral loans	3,246,399
Holders of Bonds/Private Notes	3,415,541
Sub Total	6,661,934
Grand Total	28,869,418

Source: *Data supplied by the Debt Management Office, Abuja, Nigeria.*

The currency composition of Nigeria's external debt has varied over the years. The currency composition of long-term external debt between 1970 and 1998 is shown in table 4. In 1970, multiple currencies dominated with a share of about 39 percent, followed by pound sterling with a share of about 30 percent.

By 1980, dollars had a share of 55 percent in long-term debt, followed by the Deutsche mark with a share of about 24 percent. By 1998, the dollar share in total long-term debt declined to about 31 percent, followed by the Japanese yen and the pound sterling with about 12.9 percent and 12.6 percent respectively.

Table 4: Nigeria: Currency Composition of Long Term Debt: 1970 - 98

	1970	1980	1993	1994	1995	1996	1997	1998
Deutsche Mark	9.0	23.5	12.8	13.3	14.2	11.1	10.9	11.2
French Franc	0.0	0.9	10.2	10.4	10.9	10.7	10.2	10.5
Japanese Yen	0.8	2.0	12.6	13.3	12.6	12.0	11.9	12.9
Pound Sterling	30.4	2.7	10.2	10.0	9.9	11.9	13.0	12.6
Swiss Franc	0.3	0.4	0.5	0.5	0.6	0.5	0.5	0.6
Multiple Currency	38.5	12.1	12.1	11.8	11.5	10.9	10.5	9.8
Official Drawing Rights	0.0	0.0	0.0	0.0	0.0	0.0	0.1	0.2
Other Currencies	11.1	3.4	9.0	10.2	10.7	11.4	11.0	10.9
Dollar	9.9	55.0	32.6	30.5	29.6	31.5	31.9	31.3

Source: World Bank, *Global Development Finance, 2000.*

As mentioned earlier, the debt burden of a country inevitably imposes a number of constraints on its growth prospects. The burden of principal, interest payments, and other payments, for example, drains the nation's resources and curtails the possible expenditure of resources on other productive ventures. To appreciate the magnitude of the problem, shown in table 5, is the external debt outstanding/debt service by borrower category for the years 2000–05. The total debt service is expected to rise from about US$0.08 billion to about

US$1.0 billion in 2005. The disbursed outstanding debt will, however, fall from US$20.7 billion at the end of 2001 to US$5.2 billion at the end of 2005.

Table 5. External Debt Outstanding/Debt Service Payments by Borrower Category 1 for Calendar Years 2000–05 (in Thousands of U.S. Dollars)

All Loans	2000	2001	2002	2003	2004	2005
CENTRAL GOVERNMENT						
Disbursed Outstanding Debt	19,557,906	7,767,548	7,200.480	6,553.016	5,874.059	5,182.728
Total Debt Service	79,481	1,220,525	1,082,063	1,048,134	1,048,134	986,631
PUBLIC CORPORATIONS						
Disbursed Outstanding Debt	1,099,993	394,279	259,860	58,779	119.318	43,228
Total Debt Service	4,695	202,165	166,310	66,440	156,225	18,631
PRIVATE SECTOR						
Disbursed Outstanding Debt	47,136	0	-	-	-	-
Total Debt Service	-	5,693	-	-	-	-
TOTAL						
Disbursed Outstanding Debt	20,705,036	9,161,827	7,460,340	5,932,837	5,932,837	5,225,956
Total Debt Service	94,177	1,428,382	1,248,374	1,204,389	1,080,195	1,005,262

Source: *Data supplied by the Debt Management Office, Abuja, Nigeria.*

Causes of External Debt Accumulation

The next logical question to ask is why has Nigeria accumulated so much external debt over the years. There is no shortage of literature on the causes of the developing country's debt crisis (Ajayi and Khan 2000). Debt accumulation has been brought about in many cases by the overly ambitious attempts of many governments to speed up growth, prompted by international creditors who were also overly generous. The ability of debtor countries to meaningfully absorb and pay for the debts was overstated. The causes of debt accumulation in Nigeria have been attributed mainly to external and internal factors. Chart 1a gives a graphical view of the amount of external debt and debt service till the year 2009.

Chart 1a. Debt and Debt Service, 2000-2009

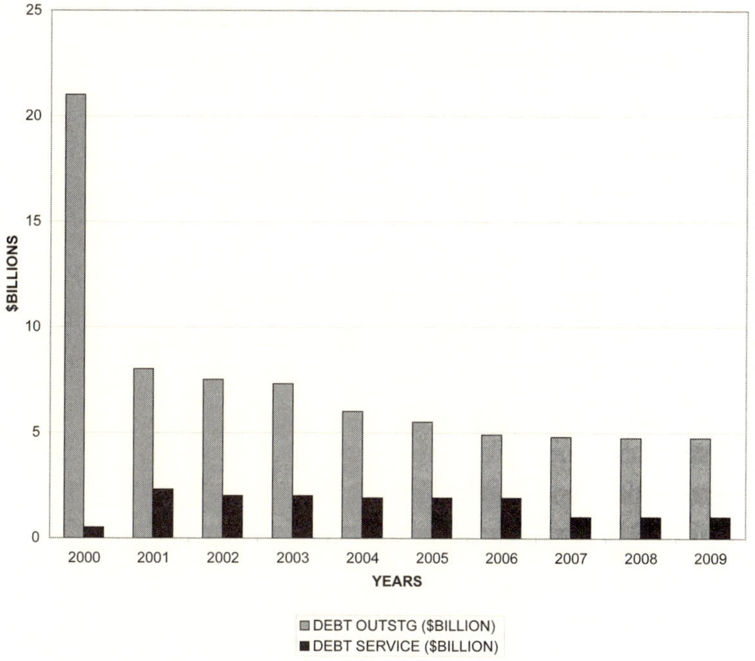

■ DEBT OUTSTG ($BILLION)
■ DEBT SERVICE ($BILLION)

The external factors include the impact of world oil price shocks, rising real interest rates brought about by the restrictive monetary policy of developed countries, declining terms of trade, and liberal lending policies of the international commercial banks. The problems arising from the external sector were exacerbated in most cases by internal factors, mostly attributed to successive administrations' macroeconomic policy errors, in addition to their penchant for investing in white elephant projects. Two of such domestic macroeconomic policy errors are those attributed to fiscal irresponsibility and exchange rate misalignment (Ajayi 1991).

External Debt Burden and Debt Servicing Capacity

The external debt situation of a country is often measured by a number of macroeconomic aggregates and debt data. These ratios generally offer measures of the cost of, or the capacity for, debt servicing. The following ratios are often used:

- Total debt service to exports of goods and services
- Total debt service to gross domestic product (GNP)
- Interest payments to exports of goods and services
- Interest payments to the gross domestic product (GDP)
- Total debt service to GNP (or to the gross domestic product)
- Reserves to debt outstanding and disbursed
- Total external debt to exports of goods and services
- Total external debt to GNP

Of the above indices, the ratio of external debt to income (that is debt to GDP or debt to GNP), the ratio of debt service to exports, the ratio of debt service to GDP, and the ratio of debt to the exports of goods and services are the most often used. The most convincing evidence of a country's ability to service its external debt is the stream of foreign exchange it earns, and hence the ratio of external debt to exports is an important debt-burden indicator.

Table 6 shows some indices of Nigeria's external debt burden and debt servicing capacity from 1977 to 1997. The debt service as a ratio of exports was about 2 percent in the 1970s. In the 1980s and 1990s, the ratio was 23 percent and 17 percent, respectively. When we take a close look at two important ratios, external debt to exports of goods and services and external debt to GNP, the picture is different. External debt as a ratio of exports of goods and services rose from about 24 percent in 1977 to about 407 percent in 1988. It declined thereafter until 1993 when it started to rise again reaching the level of 317 percent in 1994. The ratio stood at about 157 percent in 1997.

Table 6: Nigeria: Debt Burden Indicators, 1977 – 97, Percent.

YEAR	TDS/X	EDT/X	EDT/GNP	INT/X	INT/GNP
1977	1.0	23.6	8.8	0.4	1.5
1978	1.3	43.8	14.0	0.6	0.2
1979	2.2	34.6	13.3	1.4	0.5
1980	4.1	32.1	14.6	3.3	1.5
1981	9.2	58.6	19.6	5.9	2.0
1982	16.2	92.8	24.6	9.7	2.6
1983	23.6	161.5	51.2	13.0	4.1
1984	32.9	143.9	64.8	15.7	7.0
1985	32.7	137.9	68.1	12.7	6.3
1986	38.0	411.7	118.2	15.0	4.3
1987	14.1	370.5	137.9	8.3	3.0
1988	30.4	406.8	132.6	20.9	6.8
1989	24.7	350.8	138.5	17.6	6.9
1990	22.6	226.4	130.7	14.6	8.4
1991	21.9	249.9	134.9	15.5	8.4
1992	28.7	222.3	97.5	14.3	6.3
1993	12.5	257.5	161.5	7.6	4.8
1994	17.9	317.3	155.3	10.8	5.3
1995	13.9	257.4	131.7	6.9	3.5
1996	14.0	175.3	95.0	6.1	3.3
1997	7.8	156.6	75.6	3.2	1.6

Source: World Bank, *Global Development Finance*, 2000.

Looking at the ratio of external debt to GNP, we see the extent of the problem. Up until 1982 the ratio was fairly low at less than 25 percent. The ratio, however, started rising steadily thereafter, reaching about 162 percent in 1993. The implication is that external debt is much greater than the resources of the economy. Even though the ratio stood at about 76 percent in 1997, it was nevertheless a serious situation (see charts 2–5). The behavior of the indicators of the debt burden under various assumptions can also be further analyzed. In other words how do the various indicators of debt burden behave under various assumptions? To do this the growth-cum-debt model is often developed using a simple growth dynamic equation. (See Solis and Zedillo (1985), Ajayi (1991), and Ajayi and Khan (2000) for work on Nigeria).

Chart 2. Nigeria External Debt and Debt Service, 2000-2009 (US$ Billions)

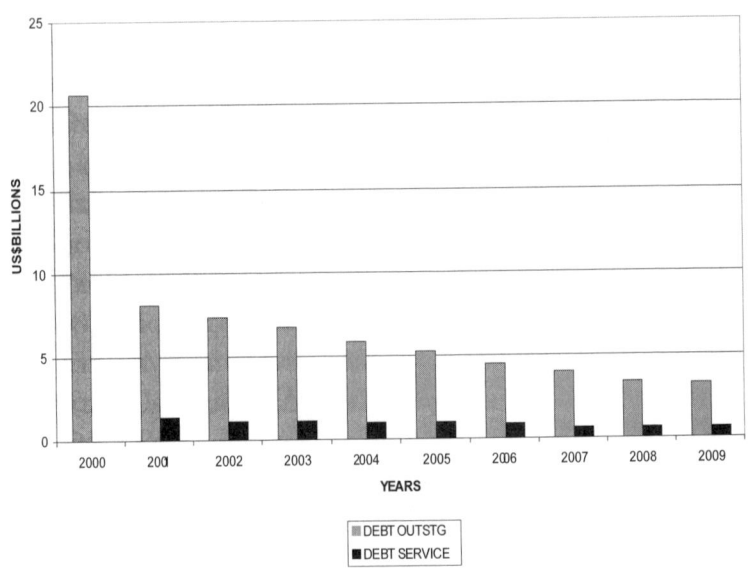

Chart 3. Nigeria Debt Indicators, 1977-97

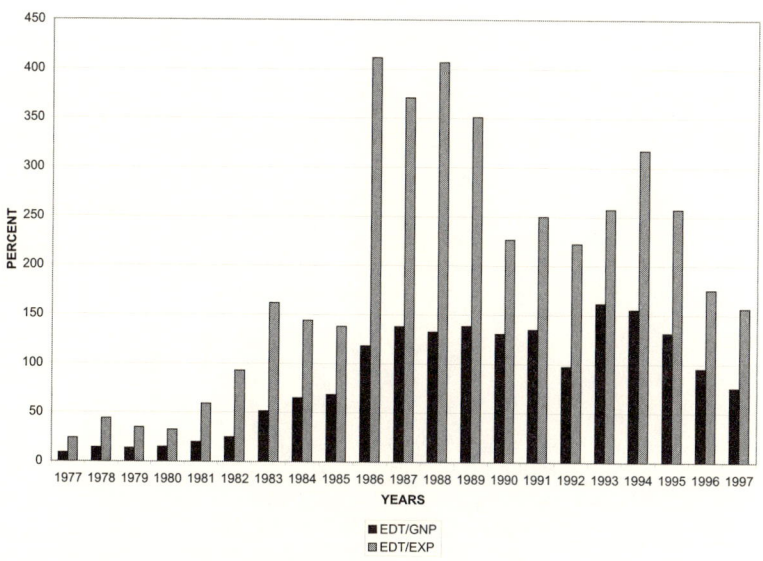

Chart 4. Nigeria Debt Export Ratio and Debt GNP Ratio, 1977-97

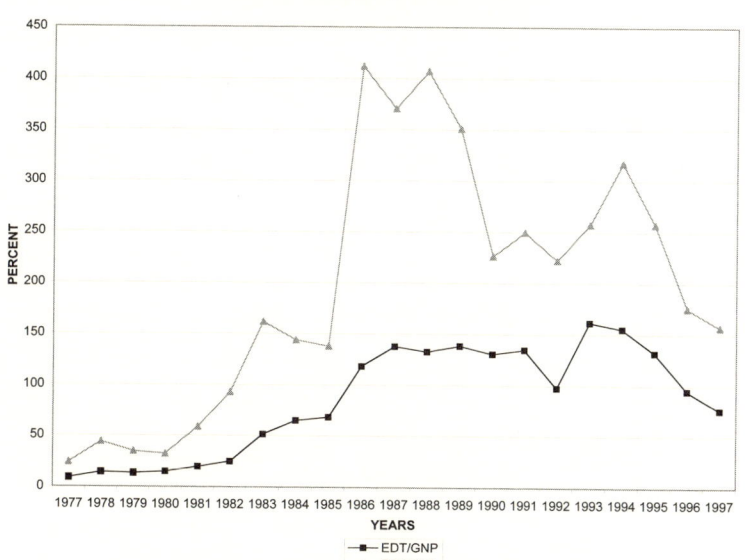

Chart 5. Nigeria Debt Burden Indicators, Debt Export and Debt GNP Ratios, 1977-97

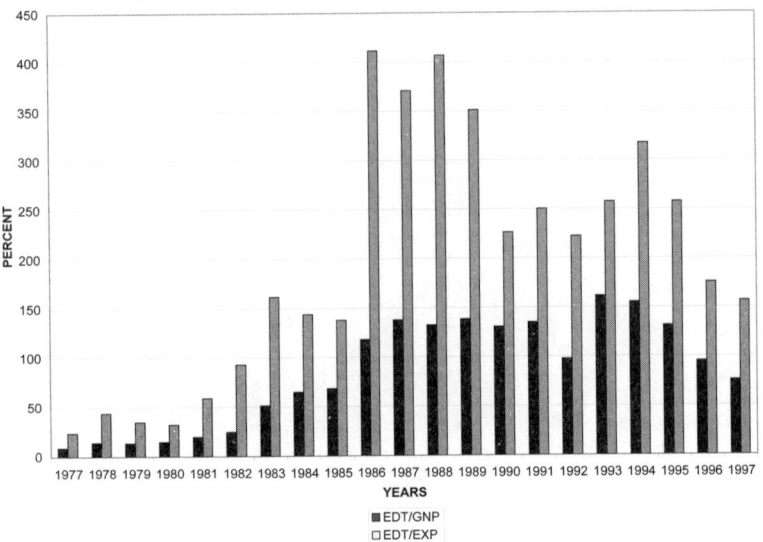

We can compare the performance of Nigeria's external debt-export ratio and external debt-GNP ratio with that of other regional groups to put in perspective the seriousness of Nigeria's external debt problems. Shown in table 7 and charts 6 and 7 are data for Sub-Saharan Africa as a group, Latin America, and the Caribbean and all developing countries. Comparing this with an earlier table on Nigeria, it can be seen that Nigeria's debt-GNP ratio was worse than the other groups in the period shown. In the case of the debt-export ratio, Nigeria fared better than the other regions as a group in the period 1996 to 1997, but performed worse than other regions in the rest of the period shown. The debt-export ratio was worse than that of all developing countries as a group.

Table 7. Comparative Burden Indicators, Percent

YEAR	SUB-SAHARAN AFRICA			LATIN AMERICA & THE CARIBBEAN			ALL DEVELOPING COUNTRIES		
	EDT X	EDT GNP	TDS X	EDT X	EDT GNP	TDS X	EDT X	EDT GNP	TDS X
1980	66.4	24.1	7.3	201.9	34.8	36.3	85.3	21.0	13.1
1991	225.6	65.9	12.5	261.4	44.1	24.2	163.5	35.6	17.0
1992	222.5	66.3	12.2	252.7	41.1	26.4	162.6	36.5	16.6
1993	246.0	73.8	9.2	254.1	40.5	28.3	167.2	38.4	16.4
1994	272.7	83.9	14.7	233.4	38.2	25.8	161.2	40.0	16.1
1995	242.7	80.9	15.4	213.3	39.7	26.9	142.7	38.2	16.0
1996	215.4	74.4	14.2	200.5	37.6	32.0	133.4	35.8	16.6
1997	201.7	68.0	12.8	190.9	35.8	35.5	129.0	34.9	17.0

Source: *Global Development Finance, 2000.*

Chart 6. Comparative Debt-Export Ratios

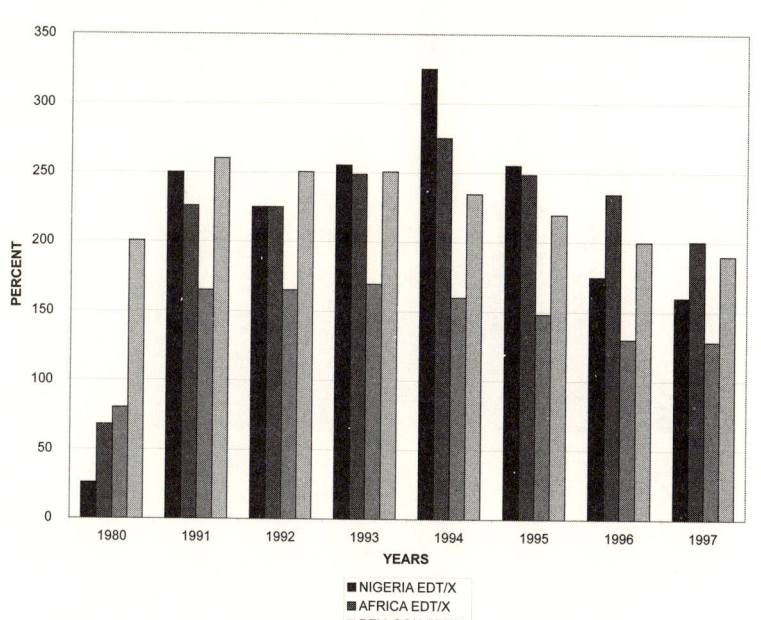

While the seriousness of external indebtedness is captured by these ratios, it is nevertheless appropriate to discuss other measures of the external debt burden and its sustainability using other criteria. We can look at the issue of sustainability from three main angles: sustainability in terms of what the debt burden indicators tell us, resource flows in the economy measured by the prospects of export growth, and fiscal sustainability. First, perhaps one of the strains and stresses in the current debt scenario has to do with the extent as well as the magnitude of Nigeria's debt reschedulingexercise.

Chart 7. Comparative Debt GNP Ratios

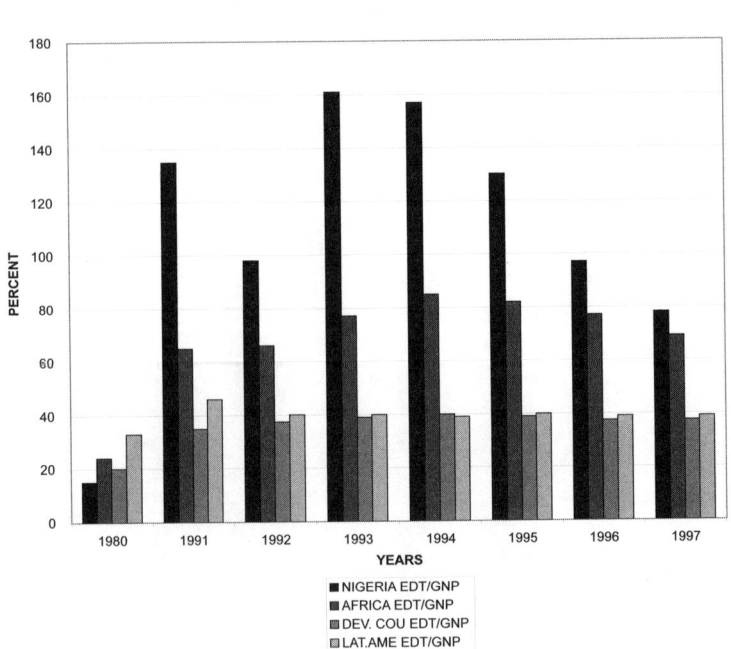

External Debt, Capital Flight and Growth in Nigeria

In 1986 Nigeria rescheduled US$5.3 billion of its external debt, in 1987 US$7.5 billion, and in 1989 US$9.8 billion. In 1997, interest arrears on long-term debt outstanding was about US$5.0 billion. Second, we can take a critical look at the growth of the economy and the export sector in particular. Over time, Nigeria's export sector has not been doing very well. Indeed, the oil is still the dominant sector.

Third, we can look at the amount of money sent away to foreign lands to pay debt relative to government revenue and expenditures. This can be thought of as the fiscal sustainability or the fiscal burden of external debt. The seriousness of the debt burden can be gauged from the proportion of the national budget which is devoted to the servicing of external debt. Table 8 shows the scheduled external debt service relative to government expenditures and revenue for Nigeria, and a number of African countries for comparative purposes. (See Table 8).

Table 8: Fiscal Measures of the External Debt Service Burden, 1994

Country	Scheduled External Debt Service Relative to:	
	Government revenue	Export of goods and services
Burkina Faso	0.28	0.18
Ghana	0.29	0.31
Kenya	0.29	0.26
Ethiopia	0.31	0.45
Uganda	0.31	0.27
Burundi	0.33	0.36
Benin	0.46	0.22
Chad	0.48	0.15
Senegal	0.51	0.20
Central African Republic	0.68	0.23
Tanzania	0.74	0.32
Guinea	0.74	0.38
Mali	0.75	0.40
Cote d'Ivoire	0.91	0.41
Guyana	0.92	0.48
Angola	0.98	0.55
Togo	0.99	0.39
Nigeria	1.05	0.48
Niger	1.10	0.39
Cameroon	1.11	0.44
Sierra Leone	1.11	0.66
Equatorial Guinea	1.11	0.39
Guinea-Bissau	1.44	0.93
Madagascar	1.66	0.62
Sao Tome and Principe	1.83	0.98
Mozambique	1.83	1.38
Zambia	1.86	1.06
Sudan	1.89	1.99
Zaire	6.08	0.76

Source: IMF, *World Economic and Financial Surveys, 1995.*

It can be seen from the table that in 1994, for example, scheduled external debt absorbed a significant proportion of Nigeria's national budget. The scheduled external debt service relative to government revenue and export of goods and services was 110 percent and 39 percent, respectively. Other countries with serious scheduled external debt service to government revenue include Zaire (with 6.08 percent), Zambia, Madagascar, Sudan, Guinea Bissau, and Sao Tome and Principe.

Debt Burden and Export Performance and Sustainability of Debt

When is external debt sustainable? The external position of a country could be considered sustainable if the country is expected to be able to meet all its external obligations in full without recourse to debt rescheduling or relief or the accumulation of arrears, over the medium term or long term and without compromising economic growth.

While the issue of sustainability is defined on case-by-case basis, in general, however, a country's external debt position might be considered sustainable "if the net present value of debt to exports is within the range of 200–250 percent (IMF Survey, volume 17, p.271); the ratio of external debt service to exports fall within the range of 20–25 percent; or for very open economies with a heavy fiscal burden, despite strong efforts to generate fiscal revenue, a net present value of debt to exports ratio of below 200 percent." Nigeria has violated a number of criteria for sustainability and has not only accumulated arrears, but has also been involved in rescheduling.

In order to examine the relationship between the debt burden and export performance it is important to remember the well-known stability condition: "If the rate of growth of exports exceeds the interest rate, a permanently positive resource gap can be reconciled with a lim-

THE DEBT TRAP IN NIGERIA

ited debt/export ratio" (Simonsen 1985, p. 103). Table 9 shows the result of such calculation. We can calculate various rates of unsustainable borrowing.

Table 9: Selected Indicators of Debt Sustainability

Year	u	u*	g	Tc	s*
1977	134.18	-83.77	0.89	1.07	-0.77
1978	75.22	-365.97	-11.41	0.78	11.25
1979	-51.26	-159.93	21.53	1.68	-20.80
1980	-7.31	-575.85	12.95	1.56	-12.45
1981	59.37	-498.13	-24.89	0.85	24.58
1982	36.98	70.07	-38.53	0.76	38.21
1983	61.67	77.38	-40.70	0.85	40.55
1984	-13.34	-16.30	6.72	1.27	-6.58
1985	-1.34	-2.11	-3.67	1.41	3.73
1986	78.27	84.07	-277.97	1.28	277.38
1987	-12.24	-11.29	127.72	1.88	-127.29
1988	8.72	11.02	-57.98	1.46	57.92
1989	-12.80	-16.58	26.27	1.88	-26.12
1990	-62.71	-69.41	152.09	2.43	-151.35
1991	10.58	8.92	-40.95	1.33	40.84
1992	-10.35	-0.72	-17.08	1.46	17.05
1993	22.44	21.25	-52.21	1.32	52.04
1994	13.34	13.77	-41.97	1.27	41.91
1995	-262.13	-262.31	681.72	0.99	-679.07
1996	-82.73	-91.18	131.62	2.33	-130.87
1997	-4.36	-17.68	-8.14	1.47	8.08

u = Unsustainable borrowing defined as the excess of the percentage growth rate of debt over that of the percentage growth rate of exports.

u* = Unsustainable borrowing defined as the excess of the percentage growth rate of net debt over that of the growth rate of exports; when net debt is defined as debt minus international reserves.

tc = Transfer coefficient defined as the ratio of value of exports over imports.

g = $(x-i)Z$ – where x is the growth rate of exports, i is the interest rate and Z is the debt export ratio.

s* = Sustainability index defined as $s^* = (i-x)z$ $(1+x)$

Source: Author's calculation based on data from IMF, *International Finacial Statistics, 1999.*

We can calculate the rate of unsustainable borrowing as the excess of the percentage rate of growth of debt over the percentage rate of growth of exports of goods and services. Second, we can calculate the rate of unsustainable debt as the growth of net debt over exports of goods and services. The calculations in the table reveal some interesting stories. First, unsustainable borrowing occurred for most of the period using either U or U* (as defined in the table).

Second, even though there was a decline in Nigeria's level of indebtedness in 1997, the level or borrowing was nevertheless, unsustainable. For the growth of exports greater than the interest rate, g should be positive. In this case, resource gaps can be sustained indefinitely without pushing the economy into relative over-indebtedness (Simonsen 1985). As can be seen, the value of g is mostly negative. The value of s* is in most cases negative. In conclusion, the stability of the debt-export ratio in the long run requires that the rate of growth of exports be higher than the rate of interest on external debt.

Thus the rate of interest at which new loans are contracted is important. The rate of interest in most cases is outside the control of the borrower, since the rate is determined at the international market where the borrower has little or no say. The other parameter of interest is exports whose growth can be influenced domestically, depending on the kinds of macroeconomic policy being pursued as well as by a favorable international environment.

The Issue of Capital Flight

Capital flight is becoming increasingly important because of its magnitude and resource flow implications, especially at a time when developing countries in general are looking for financial resources for development (Ajayi 1999). Usually, capital is expected to move from resource surplus countries to countries where resources are scarce. Any movement in the opposite direction is perverse. Many reasons are often adduced for capital flight. While the preponderant causes are economic, there are nevertheless some political factors at play. The economic reasons include macroeconomic policy errors or distortions. These distortions manifest themselves in large public sector deficits, slow growth of the economy, exchange rate misalignment, and financial repression.

Additional to these are the incentives provided by foreign banks and governments. The capital flight phenomenon is not new to Nigeria. The available empirical analyses of the determinants of capital flight in Nigeria demonstrates clearly that capital flight is caused by a host of factors including exchange rate misalignment, poor growth of the economy, real interest rate differential, fiscal deficit of government (Ajayi 1992).

Capital flight is ordinarily difficult to measure. The literature on the definition, causes, and mechanism of capital flight is vast and no attempt is made here to get into all the various issues. (Readers can consult, for example, Khan and Ul Haque (1987), Ajayi and Khan (2000), Lessard and Williamson (1987), and Cuddington (1986).) The measurement of capital flight is "fishing in muddy water" (Ajayi 1999) and a very difficult exercise simply because those who are engaged in it do not make their intentions known by informing the compilers of the balance of payments statistics (Lessard and Williamson 1987).

It is therefore a serious detective statistical work to find all the necessary information. There are many ways of measuring capital flight. Here we have used the "hot method approach" and the "residual approach" for the calculation. Other methods of calculating capital flight can be found elsewhere. See Ajayi (1992), Dooley (1988), and Cuddington (1986). Table 10 shows the magnitude of capital flight for the period from 1981 to 1997.

Table 10. Capital Flight Estimates, 1980 – 97 (US$ Billions)

Year	HM	Kf1	Kf2
1980	0.606	14.782	5.738
1981	0.191	-8.695	2.26
1982	-0.008	-8.309	-3.956
1983	-0.087	1.363	2.518
1984	-0.272	0.98	0.076
1985	3.829	2.206	1.418
1986	1.226	3.518	4.892
1987	0.1731	6.285	6.385
1988	0.957	4.428	5.572
1989	0.124	3,766	1.497
1990	0.561	7.707	2.89
1991	1.637	4.504	3.498
1992	1.2	-5.905	3.969
1993	0.088	0.992	-2.517
1994	0.139	0.346	0.297
1995	0.083	6.194	6.566
1996	0.045	9.045	2.048
1997	0.062	3.613	0.489

THE DEBT TRAP IN NIGERIA

KF1 = current account surplus/deficit + net foreign direct investment + change in reserves + change in adjusted external debt
KF2 = current account surplus/deficit + net foreign direct investment + change in adjusted debt + change in total reserves minus gold + changes in foreign assets of banks
HM = Hot money defined as
= -(g+C)
where g = net errors and omissions in the BOP statistics
C = other assets

Various macroeconomic relationships of capital flight have been calculated. These are shown in tables 11 and 12

Table 11: Cumulative Capital Flight to Macroeconomic Aggregates, 1997, Percent

	HM	KF_2	KF_1
Capital Flight (cumulative) to exports, 1997	18.60	82.30	76.92
Capital Flight (cumulative) to GNP, 1997	27.99	123.85	115.75
Capital Flight (cumulative) to Debt, 1997	37.16	123.85	115.75

Source: Author's Calcualtion

As can be seen from the tables, the amount of capital flight (cumulative) from Nigeria has varied from US$10.5 billion to US$46.69 billion in the period from 1980 to 1997.

Table 12. Nigeria's Capital Flight and Other Macroeconomic Aggregates

Year	Kf1/exp (Percent)	Kf2/exp (Percent)	Debt $ Billions	Gnp $ Billion	Kf1/debt (Percent)	Kf1/gnp (Percent)
1980	22.10	56.85	8.9	61.1	64.47	9.39
1981	12.66	-48.73	11.4	58.4	19.82	3.87
1982	-32.47	-68.19	12.0	48.7	-32.97	-8.12
1983	24.31	13.16	17.6	34.4	14.31	7.34
1984	0.64	8.27	17.8	27.4	0.43	0.38
1985	11.28	17.58	18.6	27.4	7.61	5.17
1986	94.90	68.24	22.2	18.8	22.04	26.02
1987	86.69	85.34	20.0	21.0	22.02	30.40
1988	81.05	64.41	29.6	22.3	18.82	24.99
1989	19.02	47.85	30.1	21.8	4.97	6.87
1990	21.14	56.38	33.4	25.8	8.65	11.29
1991	28.52	36.73	33.5	24.9	10.44	14.05
1992	33.39	-49.68	29.0	29.8	13.69	13.32
1993	-25.38	8.89	30.7	19.0	-8.20	-13.25
1994	3.17	3.69	33.1	21.3	0.90	1.39
1995	19.21	18.12	34.0	25.9	19.31	25.35
1996	3.42	15.11	31.4	33.1	6.52	6.19
1997	0.86	6.37	28.4	37.7	1.72	1.30

Source: IMF (1999) and World Bank (2000).

Depending on the methodology of calculation the ratio of cumulative capital flight to exports varied between 18 percent and 82 percent. Capital flight (cumulative) to GNP was significant from 27 percent to 123 percent. On a yearly basis the capital flight/debt was significant at 65 percent in 1980, and was more than 20 percent in a number of periods. The capital flight-GNP was also significant over the years.

External Debt and Capital Flight: Is There Any Linkage?

Some economists have argued that there is no causal relationship between external debt and capital flight, while others have detected a relationship. The Morgan Guaranty Trust Company (1986, p. 15) declares that the simultaneous occurrence of debt accumulation and capital flight in the third world "was no coincidence," since "the policies and track records that engineered capital flight also generated demands for foreign credit." In the case of the Philippines, the relationship between external debt and capital flight is likened to that of a revolving door. A substantial amount of foreign borrowing has been shown to be positively correlated with capital flight (Boyce, 1990).

Two hypotheses have gained currency in the literature. The first is that it is government that engages in foreign borrowing while the private sector shifts its funds abroad. The drain on foreign exchange resources through capital flight however creates a greater need for government to borrow externally. The second hypothesis, originally proposed by Khan and Ul-Haque (1985), argues that the perceived risk of investment in developing countries is higher than elsewhere.

Residents with investments at home face additional risks on their investments than elsewhere. *Expropriation risk* is one. Domestic residents face the possibility of their assets being expropriated by government through outright nationalization, taxes, or exchange controls, whereas the risks on similar assets abroad are negligible or nonexistent. An exogenous or policy-induced shock that raises the perceived level of risk could, therefore, result in capital flight; and government will be forced at the same time to go abroad not only to borrow the original imbalance in its budget but also the loss of resources that has been induced by capital flight.

The relationship between external debt and capital flight can be addressed from two perspectives. The first is in terms of the macroeconomic relationship between external debt and capital flight, and the second is strictly in terms of the causal relationship between them. The argument from the first perspective has been put forward in the preceding section. The basic elementary argument is that when capital flees a country, that amount of money is potentially for investment in productive activity. This would have earned foreign exchange if such investments were made in the tradable sector of the economy and generate through the multiplier effect the necessary growth in the economy.

One popular call is, therefore, for capital flight reversal. The heavily indebted countries will be in a better position if funds held abroad (in form of capital flight) are returned, since such funds can be used to boost domestic investment and thereby enhance debt-servicing capacity. From the second perspective, the linkages between external debt and capital flight run in both directions (Boyce 1990). Two of the linkages are worthy of note. The first is debt-driven capital flight and the second is flight-driven external borrowing (Ajayi 1997).

In the first case, as a result of large external borrowing

the residents of a country are motivated to move their assets to foreign countries. Capital flees or leaves the country as a result of circumstances that are directly related to external debt. These are usually expectation of exchange rate devaluation, fiscal crisis, possibility of a crowding out of domestic capital, and avoidance of taxes and expropriation risk.

In the second case, flight-driven external borrowing arises when as a result of the extent of capital flight the domestic economy has to fill a gap in the resource requirements of the economy, and this is filled by external loans.

External Debt, Capital Flight, and Growth: Theoretical Framework

Both external debt and capital flight can affect the economic performance of a country. There is a vast amount of literature on the linkages between external debt and economic performance (Elbadawi et al. 1997; Fosu 1999). The theoretical framework through which the impact of external debt burden is felt on economic performance is through investment and/or growth. There is a large body of literature on the determinants of growth and investment in developing countries. Most econometric studies include a fairly standard set of domestic, external, and exogenous explanatory variables. Some of these studies have included debt variables.

Almost all such studies find one or more debt variables to be significantly and negatively correlated with investment or growth. One of the important arguments in this area is based on the *debt-overhang theory*. The theory is based on the premise that, if debt will exceed the country's repayment ability with some probability in the future, then expected debt service is likely to be an increasing function or the country's output level. The debt overhang acts as an anticipated foreign tax on both current and future income. Thus, since part of the future return on any investment will accrue to the creditor as bigger debt service payments, it discourages capital accumulation and promotes capital flight.

Second, there is credit-rationing effect. An indebted country is likely to face credit constraint in the international market. This is equivalent to facing higher real interest rates, which discourages investment. As a result of reduced access to international financing, this will shift the burden of financing the budget to the domestic sector. Depending on how the financing is done, it can lead to increasing inflation (if the printing of money, for example, is involved) and higher interest rates. Higher interest rates and rising inflation have deleterious effects on investment.

Third, as a result of the complementarities between public and private investment, the amount of money that is used to service debt crowds out public investment and discourages private investments.

Fourth, there is a high degree of uncertainty in the debt rescheduling exercises. Not only are some countries not too sure of what they face but a lot of time is spent negotiating. This degree of uncertainty creates instability in the pursuit of macroeconomic objectives and thereby discourages domestic investment. Disincentive effects to investment may also arise from the perspective of the investors' expectation about macroeconomic policies that are required to service large external debt. If investors expect, for example, that large swings in prices, aggregate demand, taxation of profits, and inappropriate compensation for investments may occur, then investment will be depressed.

Turning to the effects of large external debt on growth, there are both direct and indirect channels (Elbadawi et al. 1997). In the direct channel, debt accumulation expressed as a ratio of debt to GDP stimulates debt initially, while past debt accumulation (debt overhang) impacts negatively on growth. These two channels produce a debt-Laffer curve, which shows that there is a limit at which debt accumulation stimulates growth. When this limit is reached further debt accumulation impacts negatively on growth. The third channel works through a liquidity constraint where debt service payment obligations reduce export earnings available for expenditures and thus impacts negatively on growth. The indirect channel is one in which as a result of the reduction in available resources, government's ability to expand the economy is constrained, and growth is thereby compromised.

In the case of capital flight, there are a number of negative consequences, and in the context of external indebtedness three of these consequences are of great importance (Ajayi 1997). First, any amount of money sent away to foreign countries cannot contribute to domestic investment. Thus, capital flight is a diversion of domestic savings away from domestic real investment. Kept away, these monies are also not available for the importation of the equipment and material that are needed for the growth of domestic industry and the economy. Second, income and wealth, which are held abroad, are outside the purview of domestic authorities and therefore cannot be taxed. Thus potential government revenue is reduced, constraining the debt servicing capacity of government debt (Ajayi 1992). As a result of the shifting of private wealth beyond the government's tax jurisdiction, the tax burden is shifted from capital to less mobile factors, such as land and labor. Such a shift in the tax burden is likely to be regressive (Deppler and Williamson).

Third, income distribution is negatively affected by capital flows. The poor citizens in the African countries are subjected to austerity measures in order to pay for external debt obligations to international creditors, who in turn pay interest to citizens from these countries with assets abroad (Pastor 1990).

Model of External Debt, Capital Flight, and Growth

We have discussed at length the effects that capital flight and external debt can have on investment and hence on the growth of the economy. There should be a way of linking up the issues of external debt, capital flight, and investment (and hence growth). Given the discussions earlier we can specify a simple but adequate model that captures the relationship between external debt, capital flight, and growth in Nigeria.

The central argument that is made is that both capital flight and external debt have deleterious effects on investment and through it on growth. Taking advantage of what is in the literature, and, in particular, in Blejer and Khan (1984), Fischer (1993), Fry (1993), Greene and Villanueva (1991), Serven and Solimano (1993), and Fosu (1999), the candidates for inclusion as variables in the investment equation are many, and include exchange rate, debt burden indicators, and rate of change of prices. Given the focus of our interest to take account of the capital flight phenomenon, the specification to be utilized will inevitably be different. We want to be able to test for two hypotheses with regards to the influence of external debt on investment. The first is the debt overhang hypothesis and the second is the liquidity constraint hypothesis (Fosu 1999).

In the first hypothesis, high external debt acts as a tax on future output and reduces the incentives for saving and investment. A negative relationship is therefore expected between the indicators of external debt burden and investment. The liquidity constraint hypothesis or the crowding out effect implies that the resources utilized to service debt reduce the amount of resources available for investment purposes. Thus, a binding liquidity constraint on external debt would produce a negative effect on investment (Fosu 1999). In the case of capital flight, we have argued earlier that capital flight constitutes a leakage from the system, and that the money if left in the domestic economy could be used for investment purposes.

With the points above in mind, we can specify an investment equation. Investment, the dependent variable, is expressed as a function of the black market premium (*BPREM*) defined as a ratio of the official to the black market rate to capture the influence of the exchange rate, the debt-gross domestic product ratio (*DEBTGDP*) capturing the debt overhang. The other debt overhang variable is the debt-export ratio (*DEBEX*). The crowding out effect is measured by the debt-service GDP ratio (*TDSGDP*). The growth rate of the GDP (*GGDP*) is included to capture the investment accelerator effect. The extent of capital flight is measured by *Kfi*. Thus, the model to be used is as follows:

I GDP = f(*BPREM, DEBTGDP, TDSGDP, KFi, GGDP*)

If there is indeed a debt overhang, we will expect the external debt burden indicators included in the model to be negative. Similarly, if there is a crowding out effect, we will also expect the *TDSGDP* variable to be negative. We have been limited by data availability, and the period of coverage is therefore restricted to 1980 to 97. *Ln* stands for log, the *t* values are in parenthesis under the coefficient of the relevant variables. The results of the estimations are as follows:

Ln (IGDP) = 3.734 - 0.548LnBPREM - 0.185Ln DEBTGDP - 0.158LnTDSGDP
   (18.829) (-5.154)   (-2.915)   (-1.833)
   -0.045KFI
   (-2.602)
Adjusted R squared = 0.775   *D.W. = 2.11*

The coefficients of the black premium, debt-gross domestic product, and capital flight are statistically significant at more than 5 percent. The crowding out effect variable is nearly significant at the 5 percent level. Given the value of the adjusted *R* squared, the variables included explain about 77 percent of the variation in the investment GDP ratio. The elasticity of investment with respect to capital flight, *debtgdp*, and *tdsgdp* are 0.045, 0.185, and 0.158, respectively. This means that a 1 percent rise in capital flight, for example, will reduce investment as defined by 0.5 percent. When we try to capture the investment accelerator effect, by including the GGDP we discovered that this variable was of the wrong sign and was not significant. It is therefore left out. When we tried to experiment with other debt burden variable like the ratio of debt to exports, our result is as follows:

$Ln(IGDP) = 3.831 - 0.534 Ln BPREM - 0.144 Ln DEBEX - 0.204\ TDSGDP - 0.052 KFI$

(10.171) (-3.782)   (-1.462)   (-1.748)   (-2.528)

Adjusted R squared = 0.681   D.W. = 1.85

In the above equation, the variable *DEBEX* though of the right sign is not significant at the 5 percent level. There is still a crowding out effect of the debt service payments, while capital flight retains its strong negative effect on investment. In order to take care of autocorrelation, another equation was also estimated to take care of the low value of the D.W. We have:

$Ln(IGDP) = 3.527 - 0.519 Ln BPREM - 0.092\ In DEBEX - 0.200 Ln\ TDSGDP$

(5.859) (-3~201)   (-0.733)   (1.521)

$- 0.050 Ln\ KF1 + 0.152 AR(1)$

(-2.207)   (0.501)

Adjusted R squared = 0.553   D.W. 1.998

Again, although the *DEBEX* variable has the right sign, it is not significant. The capital flight variable and exchange variables are significant at the 5 percent level. From the above results we are able to justify the existence of the debt overhang hypothesis, and the liquidity constraint hypothesis as measured by the debt-GDP ratio and the debt-service-GDP ratio, respectively, and the negative effect of capital flight on investment and hence on growth.

Managing Nigeria's External Debt

Given the importance of external debt and its impact on the national economy, it is important that attention be paid to its management. It is necessary to watch closely the resources of the economy. The reason for the close watch on external debt can be attributed to two main factors. First, debt management often has a priority claim on the resources of the economy. Second, debt management plays an important role within the overall development strategy of a country, simply because an erratic and uneven debt demands and repayments can undermine long-term development strategy. There are anecdotal evidences that many countries run into big problems because of their inability to manage their debt properly. Some analysts have claimed that the persistence of the external debt problem in Nigeria can be directly attributed to imprudent borrowing policies, to utilization of debt proceeds on white elephant projects, and to poor debt management policy.

The proper management of external debt is important for the prevention of debt crisis and unsustainable debt situation. As a continuous framework debt management involves, among others, an estimate of foreign exchange earnings, sources of external finance, projected returns on the investment the loan is financing, the repayment schedule, and debt service burden; choice of debt instruments, the amount to be borrowed, the currency composition, and the terms of the debt service; and an assessment of the country's capacity to service existing debt and a judgment as to the desirability or otherwise of contracting further loans.

The issue of debt accumulation needs to be seen within the overall context of macroeconomic framework within which debts are accumulated. Thus, debt management is seen not as a fire fighting tactic (that is at the need arises) or exigencies of the period but rather as a general policy of macroeconomic growth and development, which is proactive.

Managing Nigeria's external debt requires a gamut of technical and institutional arrangements. The institutional arrangements include administrative, organizational, legislative, accounting, and monitoring aspects of managing both the old and new stock of debt. Legislation is necessary to regulate borrowing, while the administrative framework is necessary for the negotiation of loan, its use and the making of payments when due in order not to accommodate unnecessary arrears.

The technical aspect of debt management involves not only estimating the required external loan (debt), but also examining the conditions of borrowing to ensure that it is consistent with the future debt servicing capacity of the country. Of great importance as part of the technical aspect of debt management is statistical database. There is need to develop an up-to-date database with information on how much is owed, on a loan by loan basis as well as an identification of all transactions on each loans.

Solution to External Debt?

The issue of external debt has to be seen from two perspectives. The first is from the angle of the policies within the domestic economy while the other has to be seen within the context of debates taking place at the various international meetings and discussions dealing with external debt issues. For Nigeria to grow out of debt, it must attempt to put its house in order. There are various aspects of this. The first is that Nigeria must grow. This is the key. For Nigeria to grow it must address seriously the various aspects of factors responsible for growth. This will involve paying particular attention to the development of infrastructures and accumulation of human and physical capital, in addition to providing a conducive macroeconomic policy environment where security of life and properties are guaranteed, so that foreign and domestic investors can take part in the development of the economy.

Foreign investment cannot come into an environment in which the macroeconomic fundamentals, peace, security, and adequate infrastructures, are absent. Policies must be put in place to foster the development of the export sector, so that adequate resources can be generated for servicing our current debt without sacrificing other important responsibilities within the economy. In this regard there is need for the diversification of the export sector from its present imbalance. In an era of globalization Nigeria cannot afford to remain aloof and to refuse to improve its competitiveness so that it can take advantage of opportunities offered by globalization.

Putting in place policies to foster growth of the export sector and the economy is important; but so is the need to have adequate debt management strategies as discussed earlier. The advantages of effective debt management policy cannot be overemphasized. Given the negative effects of debt on Africa's economy in general and the need to release resources there is need to discuss the issue of debt more fundamentally, from the point of view of the political dimension and the growth prospects of Africa. The solution to the external debt problems of Nigeria cannot be divorced from that of other developing countries, including all of Sub-Saharan Africa. The solution is complicated. In it is a mixture of sentiments, politics, and economics. All three elements have important roles to play and are inextricably interwoven, thereby offering no unanimously accepted solution to the external debt issue.

The problems posed by Africa's debt was addressed by the conference of African Ministers in 1997, in their resolution on the debt problem and its impact on Africa's Development Process (Economic Commission for Africa, 1997, pp. 6–7):

> Considering the amount of resources devoted by African countries to servicing their external debts which could be used for the development of their social sectors and improvement of their infrastructures; aware of the impact of the debt overhang on the continent's capabilities to attract non-debt creating flows, and in particular foreign direct investment; the Conference of African Ministers calls upon African countries, in collaboration with the international community and multilateral institutions to intensify their efforts to find lasting solution to the problems.

Not too long ago, the president of Mozambique dealt with the political dimension of the issue in a speech in Jamaica, delivered on September 20, 1998 (Ali 1998): "Developing countries should fight together on the issue of foreign debt and seek not reduction but total scrapping of our debt." President Olusegun Obasanjo of Nigeria has been also known to make bold statements concerning the issue of Nigeria's external indebtedness. He has argued for debt forgiveness and emphasized the importance of debt forgiveness within the context of the new democracy and the multitude of needs in Nigeria.

In recent times the issue of debt forgiveness has come to the fore at international forums discussing the heavily indebted countries. The seeming position of the IMF is that these debts are obligations that must be honored. The IMF considers calls for the cancellation of the debt unrealistic and that they raise false expectations. Unconditional cancellation risks debt relief being squandered on corruption, military expenditures, or grandiose projects with little, if any benefit in terms of sustainable growth or poverty reduction.

The position of the IMF is, of course, understandable looking at both the IMF and the World Bank as development institutions whose debts must be paid to maintain some degree of viability and integrity. While holding to that position, however, it is nevertheless important to face the reality of the situation. The reality is that a number of African countries have become much too wedded to indebtedness and are much to poor, and full payments of indebtedness may be difficult if the present economic conditions of these countries persist. Some African countries are deriving some debt relief from the Heavily

Indebted Poor Country (HIPC) initiative introduced by both developmental institutions. Nigeria is yet to be a part of this.

A number of arguments are often made against debt forgiveness. One argument is often referred to as the moral hazard argument. In its crude version is that any scheme of forgiveness will lead debtor countries to pursue irresponsible policies and lead eventually to a new round of over-borrowing. Another argument is that if debts were reduced through any form of relief or forgiveness, then debtor countries would be less concerned to pursue the objective of domestic stability and the promotion of growth.

Some have also argued that the whole concept of African debt crisis cannot be divorced from recent developments in Africa, with respect to governance issues. In particular are the levels of corruption, and the lack of accountability and transparency that have led to the mismanagement of the economy and the derailment of the cause of progress in Africa. If funds are given, what is the guarantee that such funds will not be siphoned to private coffers, or be utilized in such a way that it would do everything except foster development and growth? Given the burden of external debt on Africa's economy there is need to take a more critical and serious look at the issue of debt forgiveness or relief.

It is clear that a major attempt at reducing or canceling this obligation constitutes a significant push toward jumpstarting Africa's development. Given the fact that a significant proportion of Africa's debt is owed to governments and official institution rather than to private creditors, the prospects for a political solution should be bright. Nigeria, now more than any other time, needs some form of debt relief.

There are many advantages to debt forgiveness or cancellation (World Bank 1994). First, it will go a long way to reducing the high degree of uncertainties for both foreign and domestic investors. Second, many of the policymakers will be released from protracted and uncertain debt negotiations. Third, much needed resources will be released for Africa's development from the debt cancellation, and the removal of the elements of uncertainty inherent in the huge debt. Fourth, as a result of the release of new resources there will be growth in the affected African countries, with a spillover effect that will benefit the developed countries in terms of the demand for the goods and services of the latter.

References

Ajayi, S. Ibi. 1990. "Capital Flight and External Debt in Nigeria." Paper presented at the African Economic Research Consortium Workshop, Nairobi, Kenya. .

———. 1991. "A Macroeconomic Approach to External Debt: The Case of Nigeria." Research Paper 8. African Economic Research Consortium, Nairobi, Kenya.

———. 1992. "An Economic Analysis of Capital Flight from Nigeria." Working Paper Series 993, World Bank, Washington, D.C.

———. 1995. "Capital Flight and External Debt in Nigeria." Research Paper 35. African Economic Research Consortium, Nairobi, Kenya.

———. 1997. "An Analysis of External Debt and Capital

Flight in the Severely Indebted Low-Income Countries in Sub-Saharan Africa." Working Paper WP/97/68. International Monetary Fund, Washington, D.C.

———. 1999. "Capital Flight from Africa: Theoretical, Conceptual and Measurement Issues." Paper presented at 22nd General Assembly of Governors of the Association of Central Banks, Abuja, Nigeria.

Ajayi, S. Ibi, and M. Khan. 2000. *External Debt and Capital Flight in Sub-Saharan Africa*. Washington, D.C.: International Monetary Fund.

Aliber, Robert Z. 1980. "A Conceptual Approach to the Analysis of External Debt of the Developing Countries." Working Paper 421. World Bank, Washington, D.C.

Blejer, James K. 1990. *The Political Economy of External Indebtedness : A Case Study of the Philippines*. Manila: Institute of Development Studies

Central Bank of Nigeria. Various years. *Annual Report and Statement of Accounts*. Lagos

———. Various years. *Economic and Financial Review*. Lagos.

Charrette, Susan M. 1991. "A Theoretical Analysis of Capital Flight from Debtor Nations." Research paper 9113. Federal Reserve Bank, New York.

Cline, W. R. 1985. "International Debt: Analysis, Experience and Prospects." *Journal of Development Planning* 16: 27 – 37.

Conesa, E. R. 1987. "The Causes of Capital Flight from Latin America." Washington, D.C.: Inter-American Development Bank.

Cuddington, J. T. 1986. "Capital Flight: Estimates, Issues and Explanations." Princeton, N.J.: Princeton

University Press.

Deppler, M. A. and Martin Williamson, 1997 "Macroeconomic Determinant of Capital Flight: An Econometric Investigation," in *Capital Flight and the Third World*, ed. D.R. Lessard and J. Williamson. Washington: Institute for International Economics

Dooley, M. 1988. "Capital Flight: A Response to Differential Financial Risks." *IMF Staff Papers* 35(3):.422–36.

Dornbusch, R. 1985. "External Debt, Budget Deficits and Disequilibrium Exchange Rates." In Gordon W. Smith and J. T. Cuddington, eds., *International Debt and the Developing Countries: A World Bank Symposium*.Washington, D.C.: World Bank.

————. 1986a. "International Debt and Economic Instability." Paper presented at the symposium on Debt, Financial Stability, and Public Policy, Federal Reserve Bank of Kansas City, Jackson Hole, Wyoming, August 27—29, 1986.

————. 1986b. *Dollars, Debts and Deficits*. Cambridge, Mass.: MIT Press.

Economic Commission for Africa (ECA). 1997. *Financial Sector Reforms and Debt Management in Africa: Proceedings of the Sixth Session of the Conference of African Ministers of Finance*.

Dornbusch, R., and F. L. C. H. Helmers, eds. 1988. *The Open Economy: Tools for Policy Makers in Developing Countries*. New York: Oxford University Press.

Elbadawi, Ibrahim 1997. "Debt Overhang and Economic Growth in Sub-Saharan Africa." In Zubair Igbal and Ravi Kanbur, eds., *External Finance for Low-Income Countries*. Washington, D.C.: International Monetary Fund.

Fosu, A. K. 1999. "The External Debt Burden and Economic Growth in the 1980s: Evidence from Sub-Saharan Africa." *Canadian Journal of Development Studies* 20(2)

Frenkel, Jacob A., Michael P. Dooley, and Peter Wickham, eds. 1989. *Analytical Issues in Debt*. Washington, D.C.: International Monetary Fund.

Fry, M. J. 1989. "Foreign Debt Instability: An Analysis of National Savings and Domestic Investment Responses to Foreign Debt Accumulation in 28 Developing Countries," Journal of International Money and Finance

Frydl, Edward J., and Dorothy M. Sobol 1988. "Prospects for LDC Debt Management: Debt Reduction Versus Debt Forgiveness." Research Paper 8826. Federal Reserve Bank of New York.

Greene, J. E. 1989. "External Debt Problem of Sub-Saharan Africa." In Jacob A. Frenkel, Michael P. Dooley, and Peter Wickham, eds., *Analytical Issues in Debt*. Washington, D.C.: International Monetary Fund.

Greene, J. E., and Mohsin S. Khan. 1989. "The African Debt Crisis." Paper presented at the meeting of the African Economic Research Consortium, Nairobi, Kenya, May 27–30.

Helleiner, G. K. 1989. "The Sub-Saharan African Debt Problem: Issues for International Policy." Paper presented at the Second World Scientific Banking Conference, Dubrovnik, June 7–10.

Hope, K. Ronald. 1996. *Development in the Third World from Policy Failure to Policy Reform*. London: M.E. Sharpe.

Husain, Ishrat, and I. Diwan, eds. 1989. *Dealing with the*

Debt Crisis: A World Bank Symposium. Washington, D.C.: World Bank.

International Monetary Fund (IMF). 1995. Official Financing for Developing Countries, Washington: International Monetary Fund.

_____. 1998. *IMF Survey.* Vol 27. August 31.

_____. IFS *Statistical Yearbook* Washington, D.C.: International Monetary Fund.

_____. 1986. *World Economic Outlook, May 1986: A Survey by the Staff of the International Monetary Fund.* Washington, D.C.

Khan, Mohsin S. 1989. "Capital Flight form Pakistan," *Pakistan and Gulf Economist,* pp. 40 – 50.

Khan, Mohsin S., Nadeem Ul-Haque. 1987. "Capital Flight form Developing Countries." *Finance and Development,* Vol 24. pp 2 –5. Washington, D.C.: International Monetary Fund.

Kindelberger, C. P. 1987. "Capital Flight: A historical Perspective," in *Capital Flight and the Third World.* D. R. Lessard and J. Williamson. Washington: Institute for International Economics.

Krugman, Paul. 1988. "Financing versus Forgiving a Debt Overhang: Some Analytical Notes," Journal of Development Economics, Vol. 29, No. 2, pp. 253 – 268.

Lessard, D. R., and John Williamson, eds. 1987. *Capital Flight and Third World Debt.* Washington, D.C.: Institute for International Economics.

Pastor, M. Jr. 1990. "Capital Flight from Latin America," *World Development,* Vol. 18, No. 1, pp. 1-18.

Serven, Luis, and Andres Solimano. 1993. "Debt Crisis, Adjustment Policies and Capital Formation in Developing Countries: Where Do We Stand?" *World Devel-*

opment 21(1)

Selowsky, Marcello, and H.G. Van der Tak 1986. "The Debt Problem and Growth." *World Development*, 14(9)

Simonsen, Mario Henrique. 1985. "The Developing Country Debt Problem." In Gordon W. Smith and J. T. Cuddington, eds., International Debt and the Developing Countries: A World Bank Symposium. Washington, D.C.: World Bank.

Solis, Leopoldo, and Ernesto Zedillo. 1985. "The Foreign Debt of Mexico." In Gordon W. Smith and J. T. Cuddington, eds., *International Debt and Developing Countries: A World Bank Symposium* Washington, D.C.: World Bank.

World Bank. 1994. *Reducing the Debt Burden of Poor Countries*: A Framework for Action. Washington DC: The World Bank.

World Bank, 2000. *Global Development Finance*, Washington DC: The World Bank.

Part 2:
Institutional and Governance Issues

6
Sound Practices in Government Debt Management

GRAEME WHEELER
Vice President and Treasurer
The World Bank

Following the financial market instability in several Asian countries in the latter half of the 1990s, and the contagion effects that spread to several other economies, the International Monetary and Financial Committee (IMFC) requested that guidelines be prepared on public debt management that would help governments improve the management of their balance sheets and reduce their vulnerability to external financial shocks.

The guidelines were prepared in association with government debt managers from around the world. Six major conferences on the guidelines were held in the last quarter of the year 2000, and in the Middle East and Africa there were conferences in Abu Dhabi and Johannesburg. More than 300 representatives from 125 countries attended these conferences, and a final set of guidelines was submitted to the spring 2001 meetings of the Development Committee and the IMFC. The guidelines can be found on the following web sites and are available in five languages:

The World Bank:
www.worldbank.org/pdm/guidelines.htm
The International Monetary Fund (IMF):
www.imf.org/external/np/mae/pdebt/2000/eng/index.htm

The guidelines seek to identify areas of broad agreement as to what constitutes sound practice in government debt management. They cover the domestic and external public debt of central governments and the management of government contingent liabilities, but the same principles can generally be applied at the subsovereign level. The guidelines do not represent a blueprint for development. Nor are they a set of binding practices, mandatory standards, or codes. The capacity-building needs of countries differ in terms of their public policy goals, their capital market constraints, and their capacity and desire to undertake institutional reform. Nevertheless, the guidelines summarize what government debt managers around the world consider to be important elements of sound debt management practice. It is hoped the guidelines can assist countries in planning their institutional reforms.

Governance Issues

What follows are some of the issues facing governments:

- What should be their goal for debt management?
- What type of legal structure is appropriate?
- What role should the various institutions play?
- What is an appropriate organizational structure for debt management?
- How can accountability and quality assurance be enhanced so as to reduce operational risk?

The Need for Clear Debt-Management Objectives
Transparent debt management goals are essential to increase accountability, reduce agency costs, and lower transaction costs. Having clear objectives reduces uncertainty among the government's debt managers as to the strategy for managing the government's debt portfolio and deciding what new types of debt to issue. By lowering the degree of uncertainty within financial markets, clear objectives reduce the need for intensive monitoring of the government's debt-management goals.

Most Organization for Economic Cooperation and Development (OECD) governments and a number of non-OECD governments have adopted debt-management objectives aimed at ensuring that the government's financing needs and payment obligations are met at the lowest possible cost over the medium to long run, consistent with a prudent degree of risk.

A Well-Defined Legal Structure
A well-defined legal structure for government debt management is essential to avoid potential abuses of power and establish accountability for debt management. Such a framework reduces the possibility of having multiple issuers of government debt. Uncertainty, and therefore

transaction costs, will be reduced if transactors know that the government debt managers have the legal authority to represent the government and that the government stands behind any transaction that the debt managers enter into.

Debt management legislation usually refers to the government's powers to borrow, invest, enter into other transactions (for example, guarantees, indemnities, and derivative transactions), and to redeem and repurchase government debt. It usually authorizes the minister of finance to conduct all borrowing on behalf of the government and enables the minister to delegate some or all of those powers to the head of the ministry of finance or the head of the debt office.

The legal structure around borrowing decisions needs to be carefully considered because those powers are considerable, given that the government's debt portfolio is usually the largest financial portfolio in the country. Often the legislation will impose ceilings on the amount of debt that can be borrowed in any one year. The degree of procedural difficulty associated with borrowing particular maturities or accessing different instruments can also have important incentive effects on the types of borrowing decisions that the government debt managers will make.

In many developing countries, for example, the legal and parliamentary procedures for borrowing long maturity debt are complex, and debt managers may decide simply to borrow through short-term instruments and rollover the borrowings as they fall due. This can result in an excessive reliance on short-term debt and increase the refinancing risk for governments, in the sense that a government may have to refinance its debt at a time when interest rates have increased appreciably, or face the risk that it may not be able to access international capital markets at all times.

Clarity in Institutional Roles

A range of institutional locations are possible for government debt management provided there are agreed mandates, the organizational framework is specified, and there is coordination and sharing of information. In many developing countries, however, government debt management objectives are poorly specified, and responsibility for debt management is spread over four or five different government agencies (for example, Ministry of Finance, Ministry of Planning, audit department, or the central bank). Often there is conflict and competition among the different parties and a lack of trust and information exchange, all of which undermines the quality of government debt management. Even when government debt management is centralized within the Ministry of Finance, three or four different parts of the ministry could be involved, and it is not unusual for correspondence between the different parties to remain unanswered for several months.

The debt management function within OECD countries is usually concentrated in the Ministry of Finance, and one department is responsible for managing the government's domestic currency and foreign currency debt. The department may also be charged with monitoring contingent liabilities, although this may be done elsewhere in the ministry. Quite often, the debt office will have an agency agreement with the central bank whereby the central bank provides services for the debt managers on a contractual basis (for example, cash management, management of auctions, or registry functions). Irrespective of the structure, there is clarity as to the government's debt management objectives, legal responsibilities are well defined, and there is transparency as to who is responsible for providing advice on debt management policy, and the implementation of different aspects of debt management.

A number of OECD governments have set up autonomous, specialist debt management agencies outside the Ministry of Finance (Australia, Austria, Ireland, Portugal, Sweden, and the United Kingdom). Unfortunately, when considering the sequencing of their government debt management reforms, many emerging market countries begin by focusing on alternative organizational structures without first clarifying their debt management objectives, or thoroughly understanding the nature of the business and the preconditions necessary for a particular organizational structure. This also frequently occurs in respect of investment in information systems for government debt management.

Efficient Organizational Structure
Many of the leading government debt management organizations have adopted an organizational structure similar to that found in leading corporate treasuries. This structure often includes a front, middle, and back office. Typically, the front office is responsible for the analysis and efficient execution of domestic currency and foreign currency transactions and for government cash management. The middle office undertakes risk analysis, develops a debt management strategy, monitors portfolio and operational risk, and measures performance against risk-management policies. Information technology and legal services may also form part of the middle office. The back

office usually contains accounting and settlement functions, including confirmation of transactions, issuing payment instructions, and administering loans.

Quality Assurance Measures
These measures include the following types of arrangements:
- Clear procedures in respect of roles and authorities: for example, portfolio managers are not able to set benchmarks to assess their transaction-related performance and are not able to issue payment instructions to banks. Staff authorizing payment instructions should not also be responsible for financial reporting.
- Directives as to the authority of individual staff, etc.: Often, there will be formal delegations of portfolio management responsibilities flowing from the Minister of Finance to the head of the Ministry of Finance, or to the head of the debt management office. These, in turn, are sub-delegated, usually with reduced transaction limits, to individual portfolio management staff.
- Well-defined debt management strategy: This is supported by risk analysis and appropriate documentation. Portfolio management policies and settlement procedures should be documented.
- Financial accounts of the debt office should be audited by the government audit office or by external auditors. There should also be comprehensive reporting of debt management activities to the Minister of Finance or to Parliament.
- Outside advisors will be brought in to review the

government's debt management strategy: These have been used in the case of Australia, Belgium, Colombia, Ireland, New Zealand, and Sweden.
- Many of the debt management offices in the OECD countries (Austria, Ireland, New Zealand, Sweden, and Colombia) have established advisory boards that meet on a regular basis and review the operations of the debt management office. The main role of the advisory boards is to provide the Minister of Finance with assurances as to the quality of the decision making in the debt office. These advisory boards are often small in size and usually comprise representatives from both the public and private sector, although care is taken to eliminate any conflict of interest.

Government debt managers tend to face significant operational risks in three areas:

- Obtaining and retaining qualified staff with relevant financial market skills: Often there is a shortage of skills within the country in these areas, and there is frequently a high demand for such staff in the private sector.
- Governments differ in the way in which they have approached this constraint: Some governments have increased salary levels beyond those generally available in the public sector. Other governments have not chosen this course given that similar problems exist in respect of other areas where there is a shortage of staff with mar-

ket related skills (for example, government auditors and tax inspectors). Many countries have invested heavily in training and brought in experienced debt management staff on contract and assigned them responsibility for training other staff in the debt office.
- Ensuring sound management information systems, which capture all cash flows and are fully integrated into the government accounting system: This is an area where it is easy to make mistakes and large sums of money can be wasted. Often the most complex area of systems development involves the middle office, and, before making systems decisions, the government debt managers need to be clear about their goals, their debt management strategy, their desired business architecture, and user requirements.

Risk Management

Once government debt managers have established goals for the government's debt management, and have an understanding of the government's preferences or tolerances for cost and risk, they are able to undertake risk analysis and derive cost and risk tradeoffs for managing the government's debt portfolio. This is usually done through projecting debt servicing payments for a number of years, and developing a range of scenario analyses based on changes in interest rates and exchange rates (if the portfolio is a foreign currency portfolio), and different portfolio structures (for example, fixed and floating rate debt composition).

Over time the debt managers' objective will be to

transform the composition of the actual government debt portfolio closer to the preferred debt structure. This could be done through hedging transactions, if these are available, or by new borrowing decisions.

Portfolio Risk
An objective of minimizing debt-servicing costs irrespective of risk should not be an objective. What may appear to be a cheaper transaction will often embody significant risks, (refinancing risks, currency risk), constrain a government's capacity to repay lenders, and prove to be very expensive. Financial crises have often occurred because governments have focused solely on expected cost savings (associated with foreign currency loans, short-term debt, and bonds containing put options). This can leave government budgets seriously exposed to changing financial market conditions; that is, changes in country credit worthiness or global contagion.

Debt managers need to take into account the risks associated with foreign currency and short-term or floating rate debt. For example, foreign currency debt may appear to be cheap in a fixed exchange rate environment, but can be risky if the exchange rate regime becomes untenable, as shown by the experience of several East Asian economies in the late 1990s. This led to poor asset and liability management practices in the financial and nonfinancial corporate sector, and to their governments' injecting large amounts of capital into the domestic banking system.

Short-term debt that may *ex-ante* appear cheaper in a positively sloped yield curve environment, can create substantial rollover risk. In some situations it can mean that the central bank is under pressure not to raise interest rates to address inflation concerns, or support the exchange rate because of concerns about the short-term impact on the government's fiscal position.

For countries with a high debt load or which are vulnerable to shocks, managing rollover risk should be given first priority. This risk can be reduced by lengthening the maturity of new borrowings and can be accomplished by issuing floating rate debt, foreign currency, or foreign-currency indexed debt. Over the medium term a strategy for developing the domestic currency debt market can help to relieve this constraint and permit the issuance of a less risky debt structure. Governments in many emerging market economies are developing their domestic bond markets to reduce their balance sheet risk and provide an alternative source of long maturity funding over time. Building a yield curve in domestic fixed rate instruments may lead to higher debt-servicing costs in the short run. Countries that have successfully developed their domestic government bond markets include Chile, Mexico, Poland, and South Africa.

Debt managers who seek to actively manage their debt by forecasting interest rates and exchange rates should be aware of the risks, and be accountable for their actions. Judgments about future movements in interest rates and exchange rates are inherent within all debt management strategies. Most debt managers adopt the view that future currency and interest rates cannot be forecast any more accurately than by what is implied by current forward rates. An alternative approach is to assume that forward curves are not an efficient predictor of prices, and that debt managers can systematically predict the way in which market biases and distortions will affect relative prices. Most governments do not undertake tactical trading because of the risks involved.

Debt managers should consider the impact of contingent liabilities on the government's financial position when making borrowing decisions. Contingent liabilities represent potential financial claims against the government that have not yet materialized, but which could trigger a firm financial obligation or liability under certain circumstances. Once materialized, contingent liabilities can be a major factor in the build up of public sector debt, especially if the liabilities lead to large fiscal injections into the banking system. Public sector debt to gross domestic product ratios more than doubled in some Asian countries following the need for huge fiscal transfers during the period of financial market instability in the late 1990s.

Finally, governments need to monitor the risk exposures associated with explicit contingent liabilities. In some countries, this monitoring function is undertaken by the government debt managers. Governments should disclose the nature of contingent liabilities and their beneficiaries in their budget documentation. Best practice would be to provide an estimate of expected losses from contingent liabilities. Governments can do much to reduce these liabilities by improving their economic management and by prudential supervision and regulation, strengthening accounting and disclosure requirements, and ensuring that all the situations that could trigger the contingent liability are not under the control of the beneficiary, and thereby creating moral hazard risks for the government.

7
Managing Nigeria's Debt:
Institutional and Governance Aspects

NGOZI OKONJO-IWEALA
Director, The World Bank

While a great deal of attention has been paid to the size, structure, repayment profile, and economic impact of Nigeria's debt, until recently relatively little attention has been accorded to the institutional arrangements for proper management of the debt. Yet, institutional arrangement and governance structures, or the lack thereof, can themselves significantly affect the size and structure of a country's debt and its economic development in general.

A recent World Bank study on sovereign debt management[1] notes that prudent and effective sovereign debt management is important for several reasons: (a) It can contribute to the assurance of a country's financial stability and thereby help make it less susceptible to financial risk and contagion; (b) through its linkages to fiscal, monetary, and exchange rate policy, it can help assure good macroeconomic management; (c) it can also help improve a country's credit rating and lower borrowing costs for the government by "reducing the credit risk premium in the term structure"; (d) it can help develop the country's domestic financial markets and encourage foreign investment in it; and (e) "the quality of sovereign debt management also has an important effect on the government's reputation in financial markets. Sovereign debt managers represent the Minister of Finance and the government in the financial markets.

The professionalism with which the government's debt managers manage their relationship with underwriters, investors, and rating agencies or communicate on a range of public policy issues relating to the government's role in financial markets and its strategy for managing cost and risk will affect the market's judgment of the government."[2] In this context, we will take as a point of departure that effective sovereign debt management matters for Nigeria, particularly in the context of the country's effort to re-engage the international financial community to re-establish its credibility.

Context for Debt Management

In Nigeria's case it is not clear that institutional arrangements for debt management were a priority issue for successive governments prior to the mid-1980s and 1990s. This may have been because Nigeria had little or no external debt up to this time, and undertook limited external borrowing. For example, in 1970, despite just having finished a civil war, external debt was less than a billion dollars.

Chart 1. Nigeria—External Debt (1970-2001)

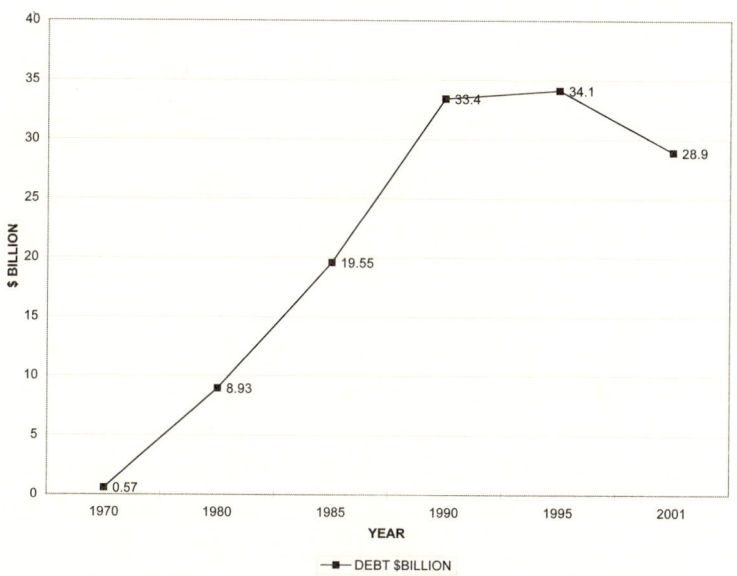

Source: World Bank Debt Tables, 1989-1990, Nigeria—DMO statistics

By 1980 this figure had increased to almost US$9 billion, as loans were contracted from both official and private sources. Following the 1970s oil shock, which proved to be a boon to a Nigeria reconstructing after the war, oil prices slumped in 1978, severely affecting government revenues and the budget, which were highly dependent on oil.

While recourse to loans had begun before the drop in oil prices, the pace intensified in an unsustainable manner following the slump as investible resources became scarcer and the then governments sought to maintain the pace and level of investments begun in the 1970s. The underlying premise for the borrowings was the belief that the public sector had to provide infrastructure, create assets, and invest in productive enterprises to create jobs.

By 1985, total external debt had climbed to about US$19 billion, much of it on nonconcessional terms. Debt service had increased to about US$4 billion a year, or 33 percent of export of goods and services (against a recommended international norm of about 25 percent). The economy was growing at a low 1 percent per annum, and it was becoming clear that Nigeria could not sustain such high levels of debt service.

The government decided to seek relief on its official debts through Paris Club rescheduling, and successive reschedulings took place in 1986, 1989, and 1991. Despite some relief provided by these rescheduling, projected debt service continued to be unsustainably high relative to the capacity to pay. In addition, Nigeria was unable to benefit from some of the new Paris Club debt initiatives, such as Naples terms designed to assist poor countries with their debt burden.

There was more success with the private and commercial debts as the government pursued a strategy of restructuring and buy backs in parallel with negotiations with the London Club of commercial creditors. These negotiations were successful, leading to a restructuring of about US$6 billion of commercial debt into Brady bonds at a substantial 60 percent discount. Nigeria has consistently serviced this restructured debt. With negotiations for a more favorable treatment of its Paris Club debts at a standstill, Nigeria stopped servicing these debts and began to accumulate arrears. By 1995 Nigeria's external debt had a large component of principal and interest arrears and penalties, and debt had ballooned to an estimated US$34 billion or about 100 percent of gross national product (GNP). For several years after this, the debt issue was pushed to the back burner, except for restructuring of promissory notes, a small amount of debt conversions, and some payments to non-Paris Club bilateral creditors.

Attention refocused on the debt issue in 1999, with the advent of the Abdulsalami Abubakar regime, and Nigeria made a goodwill payment of US$1.5 billion to the Paris Club. The democratically elected government of President Obasanjo, which took office in May 1999, drew international attention to the drag on development constituted by the external debt burden. The president made normalization of Nigeria's debt situation, including debt reduction, a national and personal priority.

To pave the way for action on the debt, attention was refocused on economic reforms, including putting in place an appropriate macroeconomic framework supported by an International Monetary Fund (IMF) stand-by program. In addition, the governance aspects of debt management became a priority. This included improved debt data recording, update, and reconciliation with creditors in preparation for negotiations. The reconciled external debt stock thus far stands at an estimated US$28.9 billion, of which US$20 billion is owed the Paris Club. Arrears on principal constitute 58 percent of the Paris Club debt, while interest, including late interest, is another 34 percent. Charts 2 and 3 display the composition of Nigeria's debt.

Chart 2. Composition of Nigeria's External Debt Stock (May 2001)

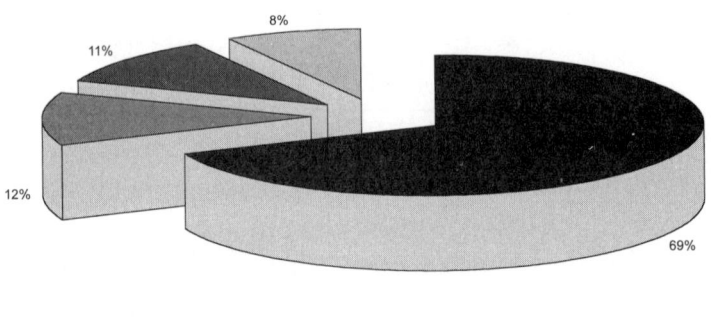

- Paris Club ($20 Bil)
- Multilateral $3.2 Bil)
- Par Bonds & Promissory Notes ($3.4 Bil)
- Bilateral Non-Paris Club ($2.3 Bil)

Evolution of Debt Management

The institutional arrangements for external debt management that the Obasanjo Administration confronted were far from good practice. There were a number of issues rendering debt management inefficient. First and foremost was the problem of diffuse responsibilities. Up to seven agencies or departments were involved in external debt management, from loan data recording to maintenance of loan documents to initiation of payments. Information flow between several of these agencies was poor, leading to delays and inconsistencies in processes. In the Ministry of Finance alone four departments were involved in external debt management.

The Department of External Finance was responsible for all Paris Club debts and for the management of all debt statistics. The Multilateral Institutions Department was responsible for relationships with all multilateral institutions, except for the African Development Bank (AfDB), and for the management and servicing of multilateral debt.

Chart 3. Composition of Paris Club Debt

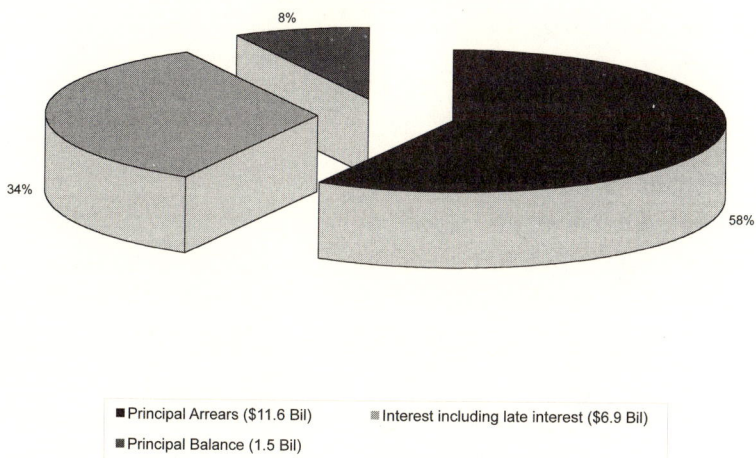

- Principal Arrears ($11.6 Bil)
- Interest including late interest ($6.9 Bil)
- Principal Balance (1.5 Bil)

The African and Bilateral Economic Relations Department had oversight for the AfDB, and all non-Paris Club bilateral debts. The Treasury Department in the Office of the Accountant-General of the Federation was key in the debt service process because it was responsible for issuing mandates to the Central Bank of Nigeria (CBN) for payment of external creditors.

Outside the Ministry of Finance, the CBN also had a debt management department responsible for the London Club debts—trade debts, par bonds, and promissory notes. In addition, various CBN departments were involved in processing and effecting loan payments on behalf of all the other agencies or departments mentioned above.

The CBN Debt Conversion Committee Secretariat was yet another small but important group whose mandate was to manage swaps through various debt conversion operations: debt for equity, debt for export, debt for nature, and debt for development. Over the years each agency developed its own approach to managing that part of the debt for which it was responsible with varying degrees of efficiency, but little cross learning.

Second, there was a problem of poor and variable debt data recording by the various agencies. Methods ranged from manual recording in the Africa and Bilateral Economic Relations department (ABER), to incomplete computerization, but with one of the best available debt management softwares (the Commonwealth Debt Recording and Management System (CS-DRMS) in the External Finance Department. Loan databases were incomplete because of missing loan records. Thus, verification of creditors' claims about past due amounts, penalties, and arrears was difficult. This made reconciliation of debt figures an issue, with the result that until recently various figures were bandied around for the total size of the country's debt. On the commercial debt side, however, the CBN did a good job of loan recording and update of the portfolio of promissory notes and par bonds. The CBN also maintained an important institutional memory on those trade debts or promissory notes that were in dispute with creditors and followed pending court cases on such debts.

Third, there was an issue of a complicated and bureaucratic debt service process. Because of allegations of fraud and diversion of payments into personal accounts, an elaborate system of checks and balances had been developed, including authentication of claims and verification of signatures at various stages. Each of the agencies with some jurisdiction over external debt would originate debt service requests for their creditors, and, as noted earlier, several departments of the Ministry of Finance and the CBN got involved in the payments process.

Each request for debt service payments had to be approved by the Minister of Finance. Exchange control approvals had to be obtained and also signed off by the minister. The Foreign Exchange and Trade Relations Department of the Ministry of Finance processed foreign exchange approvals, while the Foreign Operations Department processed and externalized payments after a final round of confirmation by the Minister of Finance that the payment could be made.

In this convoluted system, documents oftentimes passed up and down to the same departments or officials twice for verification or approval. Substantial delays of weeks or months could occur, with the consequent application of penalties amounting to thousands of dollars. Inevitably, the country's credibility on the payments issue was also dented in the process.

An interesting point is that while most debt service followed the above procedures, faster, more efficient procedures were developed for servicing multilateral (that is, the World Bank, and International Fund for Agricultural Development debts). Direct instructions went from the multilateral department of the Ministry of Finance to the CBN to pay amounts due with verification carried out ex-post. This showed the capacity of the system to work successfully with much less complicated procedures. Nevertheless, this lesson was not taken on board to effect a reform of the regular debt service process.

Compounding the organizational and process issues surrounding debt management, a fourth very important issue was the uneven quality of staff deployed in the various departments, and their limited access to equipment and resources to do their jobs. Training was inadequate and spotty, so that even the good staff had little support or incentives to maintain or upgrade their skills. It was completely anomalous that the country's most important financial portfolio of US$28 billion was being handled by less than its best people.

Two other substantive problems are worth highlighting: the issue of contingent liabilities and the lack of a debt strategy. Some of the debt service obligations falling on the federal government were in the form of contingent liabilities that had to be taken on board, but were not planned for. In the early 1980s, for example, many state government or parastatals borrowed on the international capital markets for so-called developmental projects (see Annex 1). The original idea was that many of these projects would earn a rate of return sufficiently high to enable the borrowers to service the debt. Owing to mismanagement and governance problems including outright corruption, this turned out not to be the case, and the obligations fell on the federal government as explicit contingent liabilities in those instances where it had guaranteed the loan and implicitly where it had not.

These contingent liabilities were not well tracked or provisioned for, and thus tended to have a destabilizing impact on the budget at the time of their recognition for debt service. Some of the obligations were export credits guaranteed by the export credit agencies in the OECD countries, and fell within the ambit of the Paris Club debt, while others were outside this framework.

While the magnitude of existing liabilities is difficult to quantify, it is clear that they are significant (Annex 1). Contingent liabilities have posed, and are likely to continue to pose, a challenge for debt management in Nigeria. It is possible that in future such liabilities may increase as public-private sector partnerships (which can entail contingent contracts) become more common in the economy. The government, therefore, needs to put in place clear rules of the game on such potential liabilities, and develop a process to quantify and track them systematically and to provision against them.

The second issue has been the absence of a national debt strategy linked to an overall macroeconomic policy framework and a development strategy. Such a debt strategy would provide guidance on government borrowing, taking into account the government's appetite for risk, its development objectives, growth targets, expected financing gaps, and capacity for debt service. The sources (domestic or foreign, official or private), terms, amounts, interest rate structure, concessionality, currency composition, expected uses, and impact of such borrowing would be analyzed as part of a medium-term outlook, and as a guide to yearly borrowing plans designed to ensure the achievement of the government's development objectives. The absence of a debt strategy and well-understood policies can lead to the type of situation that prevailed in the 1980s, when states borrowed in what one can only term an anarchic fashion. The severe consequences of such borrowing are evident today (Annex 1).

The 1980s borrowing was fraught with problems. There were maturity mis-matches with some short to medium loans directed to long-term development projects such as public hospitals and clinics. Loans for directly productive projects were also contracted on commercial terms, and then went to waste owing to lack of monitoring, incompetence, and outright corruption.

In some cases contracted shipments of equipments arrived, but were never installed or utilized. In others, loans were contracted, drawn down, and simply disappeared without the projects materializing. There was no guidance on project follow up, or monitoring of loan utilization by the states or the federal government, as could have been provided for through a debt strategy or other policy guidance. There were hardly any sanctions and no accountability, a situation that exacerbated the governance problems surrounding the country's debt.

The absence of accountability or sanctions in a context such as Nigeria's makes it imperative that a strategy, policies, and implementing guidelines on borrowing are clearly spelled out.

Institutional Arrangements for Debt Management: Present Status

The advent of the Obasanjo Administration has brought some welcome changes. There was early recognition that Nigeria's unsatisfactory debt situation posed a serious challenge for economic development, not least through negative perceptions on the part of potential domestic and foreign investors. Spurred by the desire to re-engage Nigeria's creditors, regularize its debt, and ultimately seek debt reduction, the president commissioned a review of debt management arrangement in March 2000. The review was completed in April, and its main findings in terms of issues have been outlined above.

The review made recommendations for a new approach to debt management based on good international practice. The thrust was the need to unify all external, and eventually domestic, debt management under one umbrella, and to better link debt policies to fiscal, monetary, and exchange rate policy.

To operationalize this, a new national Debt Management Office (DMO) was created as a semi-autonomous agency under the supervision of the Ministry of Finance. The DMO regroups the functions of various agencies previously handling external debt. In the first instance, the DMO is to concentrate on consolidating and improving external debt management. In the second phase, the DMO would take over responsibilities from the CBN for domestic debt management.

With the assistance of grant financing from the U.K. Department for International Development (DFID), the DMO became operational in August 2000 with a competitively recruited director-general at its helm. Since the DMO's inception, many of the issues confronting debt management are being resolved. The institutional framework, and organizational structure for debt management, is now clearer (see Annex 2). Responsibilities and accountabilities are also clearer, and still continue to be refined with experience. There have been significant improvements in debt data recording and reconciliation with creditors, and this work is still ongoing with the assistance of Crown Agents Consultants.

The debt service process is being redesigned, simplified, and speeded up. Unnecessary steps are being eliminated, such as the requirement for foreign exchange approvals, no longer necessary now that the debt service vote has become an "off the top," or first line charge on the budget already denominated in foreign exchange. The DMO will verify the demands and originate all requests for debt service. Once requests are approved by the Minister of Finance, the Accountant-General's office will be requested to raise the necessary mandates.

Following this, the foreign operations department (FOD) of CBN will verify and authenticate signatures and complete remaining steps for payments. Payments will still need to be reconfirmed by the Minister of Finance, following which the FOD will execute. However, the entire process will be time bound, and is expected to take no more than 2.5 weeks in total.

A DMO operations officer will monitor each step to further improve efficiencies without compromising security. Quarterly reconciliation meetings between the DMO, the CBN, and the Accountant-General's office are to be initiated, and a periodic external technical audit of the DMO's operations, including the payments system will be instituted.

The improvements already made have enabled the DMO to successfully spearhead the regularization of Nigeria's debt through recent negotiations with the Paris Club in October and December 2000. This has led to more manageable Paris Club debt service of about US$700 million in 2000, and US$1 billion in 2001, compared to debt service of about US$2.4 billion that would have been required without the rescheduling.

Nigeria has concluded many of the bilateral country agreements needed to operationalize this Paris Club rescheduling. In addition, the Paris Club has accepted to include in its agreement with Nigeria an important "goodwill clause" that indicates the restructuring of Nigeria's debt falling due after July 31, 2001, consistent with Nigeria's medium- and long-term capacity to pay, provided the government of Nigeria fully implements the agreed minutes, maintains satisfactory relations with participating creditor countries and with the IMF, and successfully completes the current program with the IMF that was approved on August 4, 2000, under the stand-by arrangement, and has an appropriate follow-on medium-term arrangement with the IMF.[3]

Remaining Agenda

Notwithstanding the significant improvements already realized or ongoing in debt management, and the resulting progress in regularizing Nigeria's situation vis à-vis the Paris Club, much still remains to be done. First and foremost is the consolidation and completion of organizational arrangements for the Debt Management Office. The three main departments envisaged in this initial phase are basically in place and functioning (Annex 2). Staffing is ongoing, along with capacity building of staff already on board.

It is imperative that incentives be adequate to attract the best people, and competitive recruitment should be utilized as much as possible. Priority should be accorded to staffing the Portfolio and Risk Management Department to provide the analytical underpinnings for policy choices on debt going forward. Recruitment of the Chief Legal Counsel and constitution of the Council on Debt Management that is supposed to provide guidance to the DMO on policy issues also require prompt attention. More importantly, the legal framework or statutes governing the operation of the DMO and spelling out its powers, need to be developed, sufficiently debated at the appropriate levels, and finalized as legislation as appropriate. This will ensure the smooth functioning of the DMO as the semi-autonomous entity it is designed to be and will further reassure creditors and the financial markets.

In the next phase, and with the guidance of its council and the assistance of the CBN, the DMO should plan for the transfer of domestic debt management functions from the CBN. This will need to be handled carefully with arrangements put in place to ensure a smooth transfer. Consolidation of all debt management in one office should facilitate better management of government liabilities, including the implications for the budget. In the past, domestic debt levels were modest, well managed, and had limited impact on the fiscal situation. However, domestic debt is now more important, with the recent doubling of the debt in 1999, from about US$4 billion to US$8 billion equivalent.[4]

The DMO and the CBN may also wish to consider transfer of the Debt Conversion Committee (DCC) Secretariat to the DMO at the same time as the transfer of the domestic debt management function, so that all debt management is truly regrouped in one office. The DCC, which has facilitated about US$1 billion in swaps since its inception, could play an enhanced role in future negotiations on debt regularization and debt reduction. For instance, the Paris Club agreement provides for creditors to undertake various kind of swaps, and this could be pushed further, with deeper debt reduction in the medium term, as creditors may again wish to undertake debt for HIV/AIDS, debt for malaria, and other kinds of swaps to meet the priority development needs and objectives of the country. A couple of issues need action and the DMO should prepare itself to tackle these. First, is the need to address the issue of contingent liabilities that already exist for the Federal government and to minimize the possibilities of incurring future liabilities. Methodologies now exist that can assist in tracking and provisioning against explicit and implicit contingent liabilities, and the DMO should be assisted to put these in place.

The second is the need for a medium-term debt strategy anchored in a well-thought through development strategy. There is a need for consensus building in the country around Nigeria's future approach to debt, and it is hoped this book will contribute to the debate and consensus building. It is clear that once the country has dealt with the problem of the present debt stock, issues of future flow will need to be considered.

Solid analysis of the direction of the economy, expected growth rates, savings rates, financing needs and sources, and capacity for sustainable debt service under various economic scenarios will help to underpin the debate. Otherwise, given the unfortunate history and experience with debt, the debate risks remaining at the level of polemics. The DMO should provide the factual basis to guide such a debate on whether or not the country should borrow, why, how much each year, on what terms, from what sources, which entity or entities are authorized to borrow, and under what guidelines and accountabilities for repayment.

The outputs of this debate, along with additional guidance from policymakers, should form a debt strategy (to be periodically reviewed as economic circumstances change) that sets out, for domestic and external audiences, the future directions of Nigeria's debt policies, including its relevance to achieving the country's overall development goals.

Notes

1. World Bank. 2000. "Sound Practice in Sovereign Debt Management." Unpublished Study. Washington, D.C.
2. World Bank. 2000. "Sound Practice in Sovereign Debt Management." Unpublished Study. Washington, D.C., pp. 13–14
3. Agreed minutes of the Consolidation of the Debt of the Federal Republic of Nigeria, Paris, December, 2000.
4. Owing to CBN conversion into debt of the over spending of the ways and means account of the last administration, the Department of Treasury has noted the sometimes unprogrammed nature of domestic debt service by CBN and the disruptive effect this sometimes had on the budget. Transfer of these functions to the DMO with the close involvement of Treasury and CBN, both of whom are to be represented on the DMO's council would help mitigate this problem.

Annex I: Contingent Liabilities: Some Examples of State Loans Assumed by the Federal Government

STATE	LOAN AMOUNT AND TERMS	CREDITOR	YEAR OF LOAN	PROJECT HISTORY AS OF MARCH 1996
ABIA/OLD IMO STATE Financing of several Manufacturing projects such as International Glass Industries, Aba, Modern Ceramics Ltd, Imo Concorde Hotel, Owerri, Umuahia Urban Water works.	French Francs 382,147,250 Plus Supplemental loan Swiss Francs 15,300,000	Banco del Gorthardo Germany Creafin S.A. Zurich.	1982	Records do not indicate how loan was split between the projects although the supplemental loan was said to have gone as additional financing to expand capacity for the Umuahia water works. The Water works was completed but only functioned partially. Many machines broke down with no spare parts. No operating capital. Regular power supply a problem. No evidence that supplemental loan was invested in additional capacity as planned. No information in the state of the other projects.
Arochukwu-Ohafia Water Scheme	Pound Sterling 12,360,000	Lazard Brother, London	N/A	This project appears not to have been implemented and loan cannot be accounted for. Some equipment seems to have been purchased.
Abia Golden Chicken Farms Ogwe, Ukwa Local Government Area	Suppliers Credit of Deutschemarks 24,457,920 Repayment in five	Lohmann Export GMBH, Germany. State Government expected to	Oct. 1986	Turnkey Build Operate Transfer after six years. BCT contract with Lohmann Export for poultry farm. Project not implemented as envisaged.

STATE	LOAN AMOUNT AND TERMS	CREDITOR	YEAR OF LOAN	PROJECT HISTORY AS OF MARCH 1996
	years with 2 years grace period	contribute counterpart funds of Deutschemarks 6,112,400 equivalent to project.		140 containers of equipment and spare parts imported and lying around project site are unused. Project said to have failed due to incompetence on part of government officials and contractors and lack of follow-through by successive state administration
ANAMBRA Ihiala Carpet Manufacturing Project	Pounds Sterling 10,039,370 Eurodollars $3,100,000	Samuel Montagu U.K.		Cross Ocean Ltd. a U.K. Company and Multi Source, Ltd., a Nigerian Company were supposed to implement this project. Neither of them delivered. Instead they are alleged to have participated in diversion of the loans into the private accounts of high government officials. Some of these officials were later indicted by an investigative panel and requested to refund the monies. There is, however, no documentary evidence that the refunds were made.
Purchase of Irrigation Pumps	US$10,633,00	Auspices of US Exim Bank	1986	M&W Pumps of Florida contracted for this project. Most of the equipment delivered, installed and functioning properly

STATE	LOAN AMOUNT AND TERMS	CREDITOR	YEAR OF LOAN	PROJECT HISTORY AS OF MARCH 1996
ANAMBRA Specialist Hospital Abakiliki and 23 rural clinics in the then Anambra and New Enugu	Spanish Pesetas 220,011,160		N/A	Infrastructure for Hospital and Clinics built. Equipment supplied to the hospital and carted away by Doctor in charge to his private clinic. No supervision or follow-through by the State Government.
AKWA IBOM Qua Steel Projects, Ltd.	Deutschemarks 73,080,000	Consortium of 13 banks led by Manuel Montagu, Ltd., London	April 16, 1981	Daniel SPA of Italy was contracted to build the rolling steel mill financed by the loan. The factory was successfully built and started production but much below capacity due to shortage of inputs. The Aladja Steel Complex was supposed to supply the 500 metric ton of billets per month needed by Qua but could only supply 60 metric tonnes. The factory closed due to closure of Aladja.
Sunshine Batteries, Ikot Ekpene	Deutschemarks 62.33 million	Kleokner Ing of Germany	1980	Loan was contracted by former Cross River State Government. Factory was built and produced at full capacity initially. But factory subsequently collapsed and closed due to incompetent management, state Government interference and closure of parent company, Sunshine of Germany which left the factory stranded for spare parts.

STATE	LOAN AMOUNT AND TERMS	CREDITOR	YEAR OF LOAN	PROJECT HISTORY AS OF MARCH 1996
AKWA IBOM International Biscuit Factory Ukang, Ikot Ekpene	Austrian Shillings 86.52 million	Austria	January, 1980	Factory began operation but subsequently closed due to Federal Government ban on wheat imports, its basic raw material. Factory extensively vandalized after closure.
DELTA Warri Farm Project	Pounds Sterling 9,578.151	Lazard Brothers London	Sept. 1993	Messrs. Rockline Ltd. were contracted to implement large scale fish, shrimp, cassava production and build a sawmill. Project was not executed. Machinery and equipment were purchased and abandoned at the site to be looted by thieves and spoilt by weather.
ENUGU Abakiliki Ring Road	US$38 million	N/A	N/A	Road successfully built but in a severe state of disrepair since 1996 due to lack of maintenance.
Rural Electrification	Deutschemarks 144,367,837	Brown Boveri & CRR AG Manheim Germany	Nov. 1977 and Feb. 1980	Project successfully built but experienced problems of vandalism, poor finances, and poor operation after NEPA take over.

STATE	LOAN AMOUNT AND TERMS	CREDITOR	YEAR OF LOAN	PROJECT HISTORY AS OF MARCH 1996
ENUGU 3 Projects: Enugu Aluminum, Ohebe-Dim; Sunrise Flour Mill, Emene; Enugu Building Materials Ltd., Ezzamgbo	Deutschemarks 95 million	Consortium of European Banks	N/A	Only one of the three projects is still operational. Sunrise Flour Mills is commercialized and under private sector management. The other two projects collapsed due to lack of spare parts, mismanagement, etc..
EDO Three Road Projects (2 located in new Delta State) Ekiadolor-Okolihua, Elume-Gbimidake, etc. Ughelli-Kiagbodor	Pound Sterling 27,647,470	U.K. Export Credit Guarantee Agency ECGD and Eurodollar		Contractor paid 85% of contract amount but abandoned roads with only one-third of the job done.
Bendel Feed and Flour Mills, Ewu and Sapele	N/A	Kreditanstatt Bankvenen Austria	May 1986	Loan contacted by former Bendel State Company is privatized and doing well.
Warri –Benin Dualization project	US$3,682,523	N/A	N/A	Contract awarded to Messrs. Road Construction Co. Messrs Nigeria Cat Company. Contract executed 50% and abandoned

189

STATE	LOAN AMOUNT AND TERMS	CREDITOR	YEAR OF LOAN	PROJECT HISTORY AS OF MARCH 1996
IMO Imo Modern Poultry, Avutu	US$32 million	N/A	1981	Poultry was built and generated funds to pay $9.6 million of the 32 million loan. Subsequently, poor management, government interference and shortage of operating funds led to its demise.
Paper Packaging Industries Ltd. Owere-Ebeiri	French Francs 95,551,848	Banque Nationale de Paris, France	November, 1980	Project was completed and began production. It was supposed to generate enough resources to repay debt and FF47.7 million was repaid. But plant now produces at 5% capacity. Mismanagement and lack of working capital are problems even under partial privatization and private sector management.
Owerri Capital City Industrial Infrastructure	Pounds Sterling 6,033 million	American Express International Bank Corporation	April 1981	Industrial layout project for basic infrastructural services managed by Owerri Capital Development Authority and contracted to Netherlands Harbor works Ltd. First phase of power supply and street lighting completed. Second phase not implemented due to lack of funds.
KADUNA Zaria Pharmaceutical Co.	N/A	International Bank Fun Aussen	August, 1993	Project successfully built to manufacture disposable syringes. Capacity utilization 35%. Suffers from competition by imported syringes.

STATE	LOAN AMOUNT AND TERMS	CREDITOR	YEAR OF LOAN	PROJECT HISTORY AS OF MARCH 1996
KADUNA Purchase of 100 Buses	French Francs 60,605,315	Banque Nationale de Paris, France	July 1987	The 100 buses were to be purchased to boost transport network of the State. Kaduna State officials claimed no knowledge of this loan.
KWARA Jebba Paper Mill (Federal Project)	US$85 million	Arab Banking Corporation	1981	This was a federal loan to build a paper mill in Jebba. Project completed and commissioned. Plant has not been producing since 1995 due to lack of working capital.
Ilorin Feedmill	Pounds Sterling 1.27 million	N/A	N/A	Plant built but sold to private company, Panat Industries Ltd. for 8 million Naira (1996) to repay debt owed to Panat. This was done without knowledge of Kwara State Government.
Kwara Specialist Hospitals	Danish Kroner 603.2 million	Private Banke	1983	Eight hospitals were built with extremely high import content leading to maintenance problems. Some of the hospitals have never been used. Most operate at 15% capacity utilization.

STATE	LOAN AMOUNT AND TERMS	CREDITOR	YEAR OF LOAN	PROJECT HISTORY AS OF MARCH 1996
LAGOS Mini-Steel Project (Lapec)	US$37.57 million	US Exim Bank	1981	Joint venture between Lagos State and Pennsylvania Engineering Co. Equipment procured and then abandoned. Project transferred to new owners with Lagos State owing 15% of the equity.
Iwopin Paper Mill	US$100 million from Morgan Grenfell US$0.1 million from Credit Italia	Morgan Grenfell Credit Italiano	1981	Project built, equipment installed but operating at 5% capacity.

Managing Nigeria's Debt: Institutional and Governance Aspects

Annex II Debt Management Office Organizational Structure (May 2001)

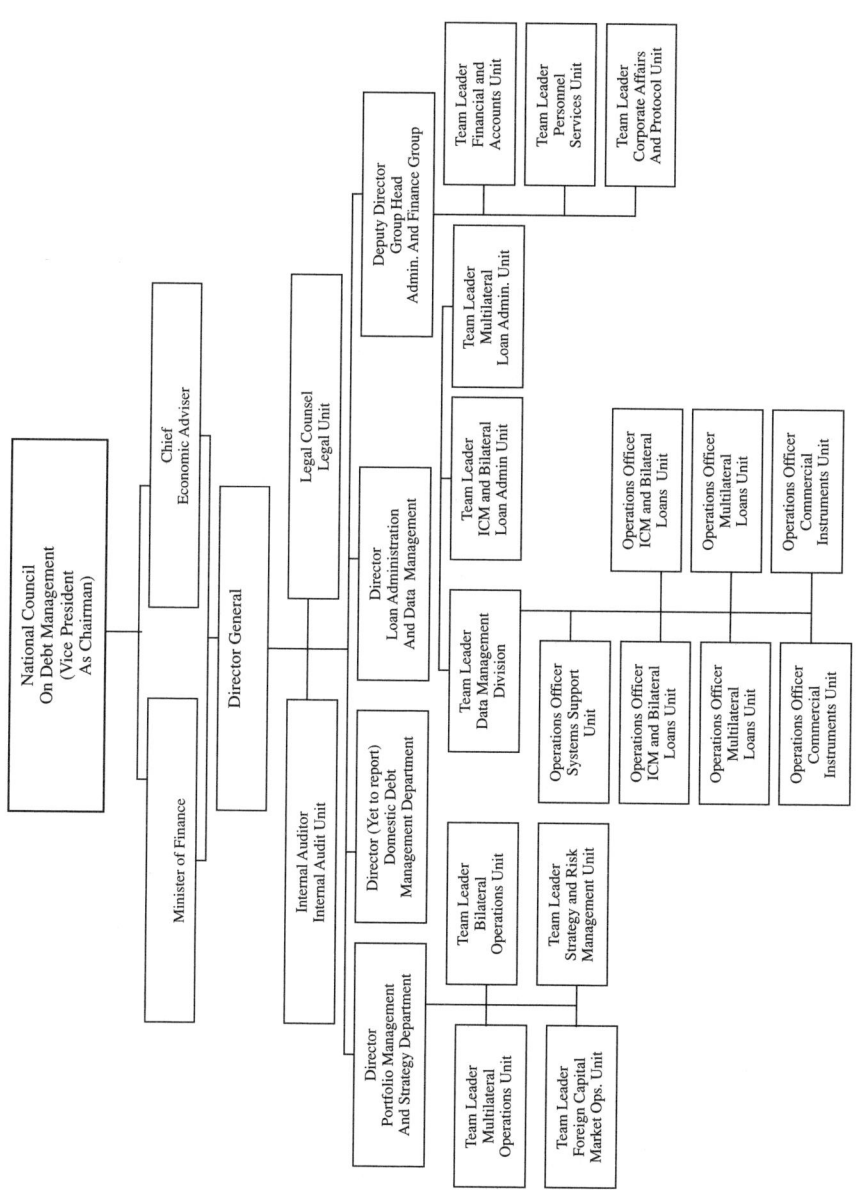

8
Toward Nigeria's Sustainable Debt Strategy

MIKE I. OBADAN
Director-General, National Center for Economic Management and Administration, Ibadan, Nigeria

That the Nigerian economy is heavily burdened by external debt is no longer news. What would, perhaps, become good news in the future is that, as a result of positive changes in institutional arrangements and the entrenchment of good governance, Nigeria's external debt is adjudged efficiently managed, sustainable, and supports development. What has come out clearly from Nigeria's external debt crisis is that the management of the debts has been very weak and inefficient. Inefficient debt management coupled with the nature of the relief packages offered by the Paris Club of creditors, have largely caused the debt problems to assume burdensome dimensions till today. The country's external debt management has tended to reflect the following:

- Continued increase in the debt stock even when no fresh loans are contracted, such that the stock increased from US$8.921 billion in 1980 to about US$28 billion in 2000
- Excessive borrowing, up to the mid-1980s, of medium-term high cost funds in relation to weak profitability and poor export earnings
- Inappropriate borrowing terms reflecting borrowing at variable and rising interest rates and shorter maturities, as well as accumulation of short-term trade debts in the 1980s
- Inappropriate debt maturity profile marked by an accumulation of debts maturing at the same time, and resulting in the bunching of debt repayments from the mid-1980s
- Inadequate information on the volume, composition, and maturity profiles of debts; even as of 2000, the question of how much Nigeria really owes had remained unresolved
- Consequently, yearly reconciliation visits to selected creditor countries of the Paris Club have been conducted by officials of both the Ministry of Finance and Central Bank of Nigeria.

Specifically, there has been no reliable information on short-term borrowings and revolving credit, private non-guaranteed external borrowing, and private sector debt guaranteed by government.

Debt Servicing Difficulties and the Accumulation of Arrears

Debt servicing difficulties, which began in 1983, have continued until now. The actual debt-service ratio—and not *scheduled* debt-service ratio—has been below 30 percent for about a decade. But this has been because of the official policy of holding down disbursement of debt service to 30 percent or less of earnings from export of goods and services. However, the ratio of scheduled debt-service payments to exports of goods and services persistently exceeded 30 percent in the 1990s, and was indeed as high as 71.3 percent in 1992. Thereafter, however, it averaged 43.3 percent from 1992 to 1997.

The ratio of total debt to exports has also been rather high, averaging 250.9 percent, although it is less than the critical value of 275 percent. Thus, the servicing of the huge debt stock has continued to be very burdensome on the economy. Given the difficulties in servicing existing loans and meeting current obligations, the external debt burden certainly looms large.

Obviously, the burden of amortization and interest payments has tended to drain the nation's resources and reduce the possible expenditure of resources on productive ventures. The setting aside of a disproportionately high percentage of export earnings to meet debt-service obligations means increasing inability of the country to pay for imports of goods and services vital for economic growth. The Governor of the Central Bank of Nigeria, at a seminar on Nigeria's debt management in October 1997 emphasized the point when he warned that the heavy external debt burden that the country is experiencing has reduced investible funds that would have aided the development process. The increasing net transfer of resources from Nigeria is compromising the growth objective of economic restructuring. This has actually been the case.

To the extent that the external debt service increases the government budget deficit financed mainly by the Central Bank of Nigeria, it frustrates the achievement of other macroeconomic objectives including price, exchange rate, and interest rate stability as well as balance of payments viability. The implication of this, therefore, is the need to reduce the debt-service burden substantially to release foreign exchange resources for funding economic recovery programs as well as make the continued contracting of burdensome new loans unnecessary. Efficient management of the debt and a good external borrowing strategy can help in this regard.

Compounding the debt position is the poor and inefficient use of the loans, thus raising issues of poor governance and corruption. Most of the loans, which were procured from private sources with unfavorable terms, were either diverted or utilized for projects that were unable to generate funds for servicing the underlying debt. Indeed, the 1996 federal government budget statement confirmed the very unsatisfactory nature of past debt management strategies to the effect that many of the projects financed by external loans are either uncompleted, or partially completed, and where they have been completed, are not functioning.

More insights, with staggering revelations, were provided into the above problem in the 1997 budget. An appraisal by the federal Ministry of Finance of 145 projects in 30 states and Abuja, financed with international capital market loans all amounting to the equivalent of $13.721 billion, with varying amounts sourced from export credit agencies (Paris Club), London Club, and non-Paris Club bilateral creditors, revealed disturbing findings and found that 18 projects, described as "failed projects," financed with credits and loans amounting to $836.17 million, were never executed. Yet the loans have been drawn down and are being serviced by government.

The implications of these findings are clear. More than 40 percent of the sampled projects were not yielding any economic and social benefits. Even those surviving projects were barely able to yield meaningful economic and social benefits. All expectations from the projects, in terms of their potential contribution to government revenue, labor employment, and the overall growth and development of the economy, have yet to materialize. Essentially, the projects have not contributed in any way to the servicing of the loans.

Essential Features of Efficient Debt Management

Nigeria's debt problem can be tackled in the context of a new policy that emphasizes efficient management, and the use of loans for export-increasing and import-decreasing activities. Three essential aspects of the effective management of debt are: knowing the debt, deciding how much to borrow, and selecting the appropriate financing strategy.

Effective debt management will enable the country to know how much foreign debt it has and how much additional debt it should contract and on what terms. But, then, how much foreign capital can the economy absorb efficiently and how much debt can it service without risking external payments difficulties?

Data on external debt have to be reasonably comprehensive in terms of size, composition, maturity, and debt-service profile, and be timely, to contribute to policymaking and to provide early warnings of possible debt-servicing problems. Information on external debt and associated debt-service payments is also essential for the day-to-day management of foreign exchange transactions as well as for managing debt and planning foreign borrowing strategies.

It is, therefore, necessary to have an active debt management unit that must continually assess the amounts of each type of credit available, and likely to be available and the impact of new borrowing on the overall structure of debt, so that maturities may be spread as evenly as possible. It will also collect, collate, analyze, and program on a continuous basis comprehensive and up-to-date statistics on external debt as an important input into macroeconomic planning and management strategy.

Effective debt management requires that the authorities must project accurately the time profile of their debt-service obligations, and forecast export earnings, domestic revenues, and future access and various sources of finance. Debts must be properly monitored to take advantage of new borrowing on better terms, to adapt loan maturities to the revenues generated by the projects financed, or to cope with shortfalls in earnings from exports or unanticipated expenditure oil imports.

Clearly, grants and foreign loans on concessional terms are the cheapest form of financing, but since these have generally become inadequate to meet most countries' needs, maximum leverage can be obtained from these loans by combining them with other types of financing. In this direction, the best mix of financing would be one that minimizes the short-and medium-term debt by including the highest possible grant element, or long-term investment or the minimum amount of market finance, and one which has a smooth time profile for debt repayment to facilitate the rolling over of maturing debt. Clearly, credits from financial markets have to be minimized in project financing.

Once Nigeria's external debt is efficiently managed, it will have the following characteristics:

- Coordination of activities both at the macro and micro levels in the country in the context of a well thought-out borrowing strategy that is consistent with development objectives, and monetary, fiscal, and balance of payments policies
- Debt-service ratio that is stable at between 20 and 30 percent
- A structure of debt that reflects all adequate spread of maturities and diversification of the sources of debt
- External borrowing to finance investments is limited to the point where the marginal product of capital is equal to the cost of borrowing
- The debt-gross domestic product (GDP) ratio is kept at a low level; a low debt-GDP ratio suggests efficient debt management as well as productive use of borrowed funds under appropriate economic policies

- The growth rate of external debt does not persistently exceed the growth rate of exports or GDP; where exports grow sluggishly, pressure would be put on the balance of payments in terms of debt servicing commitments, and high rate of economic growth and of exports are thus crucial in overcoming external debt problems
- Modern management techniques, such as computerization, are adopted to ensure solid foundation on the debt situation and proper monitoring, meaning that a comprehensive debt database is established
- The economic and monetary system is stable and borrowing policy and strategy is formulated in the context of a well-defined development strategy.
- Proper institutional arrangements for loan contracting, for monitoring loan utilization and for making debt-service payments, are set up
- A periodic review of the country's debt portfolio is conducted in view of the major uncertainties in both the domestic and external economic environment, and given the high costs often associated with debt servicing difficulties, debt management policy to include a substantial provision for unfavorable factors that could impair liquidity or even threaten solvency.

A strict adherence to the features of efficient external debt management will enable Nigeria to attain the vision on debt management as articulated in the Vision 2010 documents. It is hoped that by 2010 Nigeria will have in place efficient and effective management of loans acquisition, development, and retirement, consistent with Nigeria's debt-servicing capacity and sustainable economic growth. Indeed, Nigeria is envisaged to assume the status of a net lender of resources by the year 2010.

Desirable Debt Management Strategies and Policies

Debt Cancellation
The original market-based strategy for resolving the debt problem has gradually given way to an emerging consensus among segments of the creditor community that debt cancellation/forgiveness is a strategy worthy of consideration. This has been because of the realization that the market-based solutions have been incapable of bailing out most of the debt-distressed countries.

Debt forgiveness is the most complete and effective strategy for debtor countries to recover from debt-induced depression and resume sustainable growth. Not only is the principal extinguished, but also the steady accumulation of debt that comes from repeated rescheduling and the resulting capitalization of interest and arrears are eliminated.

Debt forgiveness would relieve African countries of the heavy administrative and financial costs associated with repeated rescheduling under the Paris Club (Greene and Khan 1990, p. 19). It is in the interest of both creditors and debtors for substantial debt reduction to be considered for debtors.

Sound Macroeconomic Management
No doubt, poor economic management and governance have played a major role in the economic and debt prob-

lems of Nigeria. The debt overhang only compounded most of the underlying structural and institutional problems retarding development. Therefore, the need for good policies and sound economic management cannot be overemphasized.

The implementation of appropriate macroeconomic policies along with debt reduction packages will ensure that debt reduction provides a much needed stimulus to investment recovery and growth. Some desirable elements of sound economic management include macroeconomic stability; boosting of domestic savings to reduce the reliance on foreign financing; a favorable investment climate and policies to promote foreign direct investment; and an appropriate economic role for government, which means that the government should do only those things that it needs to do, such as providing basic infrastructure and social services, but leaving to the private sector that which it can do best.

Sound External Debt Management Policy
Because external loans must be repaid in foreign exchange, external-borrowing decisions must be linked to a general economic policy framework that will guarantee profitability of the invested borrowed funds, and the generation of sufficient foreign exchange for external debt service. This is why it is crucial to invest borrowed external funds in export-increasing or import-decreasing activities. It is important to design a debt management framework that ensures a functional and early warning signal of debt crisis and an appropriate currency composition of external debt, and hedging to minimize exchange rate and interest rate losses from possible shifts in the

terms of trade and the balance of payments.

Authentication of External Debt Position
The authentication of external debt position is important to be able to manage the external debt prudently. This means reconciling the debt stock with creditors. This will enable the country to have accurate information as to what it is owing, so that whatever solutions that are designed to achieve debt stock and debt service sustainability will be based on accurate information as to the actual magnitude of the debt problem.

Tying New Loans to Viable Projects
Fresh loans should be sourced for projects that meet the criteria of viability and feasibility. They should be for productive and self-financing projects, which are capable of yielding economic and social benefits, including contributions to servicing the loans. Highly concessional sources should be explored for financing social sector projects.

Developing the Political Will to Implement the New External Borrowing Policy
In 1988 a pragmatic and all embracing plan for ensuring efficient borrowing and effective management of debt was unveiled. However, the political will to implement the policy is lacking.

Regular Debt Portfolio Review
Regular reviews will enable quantification and monitoring of the level of the country's indebtedness and the cost of debt servicing, ensuring that the structure and composition of the debt portfolio is optimum and have mini-

mum service cost and least indebtedness, investigation of the opportunities for portfolio improvement, and improvement of the institutional arrangements and information flow for debt recording and management

Monitoring
There is the need for proper monitoring of external borrowing and ensuring that all the guidelines and procedures for external borrowing are enforced.

Avoidance of Traditional Rescheduling Agreements in View of their Inadequacies
Nigeria should negotiate with the Paris Club of creditors for better debt relief entailing multi-year rescheduling and longer consolidation periods, debt write-offs, and the eligibility to benefit from the International Monetary Fund's (IMF) Enhanced Structural Adjustment Facility, the Naples terms, and the IMF/World Bank Heavily Indebted Poor Country initiative.

Implementation of the Privatization Program
The government should muster the will to implement the ongoing privatization program and also stop expanding the public sector into areas that the private sector is best suited to cover. If this is suggestion is heeded, then borrowing by government to finance failed projects will cease, while further losses will be minimized. The government could then concentrate on repaying losses already incurred.

Continuing with Effective Debt Strategies
The external debt management strategies which led to reductions in the debt stock in 1996 and 1997, are com-

mendable and need to be continued. They include the following:

- Moratorium on external borrowing: This was adopted on fresh loans sometime in the past. The moratorium on external borrowing by public agencies should continue particularly where the loans are not directed at export-increasing or import-decreasing projects
- Cancellation of undrawn loan/credit fund: This should be accomplished where their replacement by internal resources is feasible. The implementation of this strategy led to the cancellation of US$700 million from the existing loans/credits commitments between 1995 and 1996 (Iremiren 1997)
- Debt conversion program: This program, in 10 years of operation, led to the reduction in the debt stock by US$1.16 billion. The volume of debt reduced reflects a relatively low impact on the aggregate debt stock, and this is not unconnected with the known limitations of the program. The program should, however, be continued while taking measures to minimize its limitations
- Debt buy back: This strategy helped in reducing Nigeria's debt stock by US$3.6 billion of commercial debt in 1992 and by US$1.75 billion in 1996. The possibility of further reducing the debt stock through the debt buy-back strategy should continue to be explored
- Appraisal of the performance of projects

financed with external loans: As already noted the findings from previous exercises have been very revealing. Although the appraisal exercise is not a debt reduction measure in itself, it conjures up important lessons not only for the management of externally financed projects but also for conditioning government's attitude to future borrowing by public sector bodies. It also points to the need to use loans for export-increasing and import-decreasing projects.

Institutional Arrangements for External Debt Management

Until recently the institutional arrangements for external debt management in Nigeria reflected conspicuous shortcomings and inadequacies. As at 1993 the institutional arrangements involved three principal actors: the foreign consultants; the Ministry of Finance, which is in charge of medium- and long-term loans and public sector short-term loans; and the Central Bank of Nigeria, which is in charge of the private sector short-term trade debts.

The Ministry of National Planning had a department handling bilateral grants and loans, as well as technical assistance. The arrangement, however, tended to hinder effective debt management in that while information flowed much more freely from the Ministry of Finance and the Central Bank of Nigeria to the foreign consultants, there was a lot to be desired in the flow of information between the Central Bank of Nigeria and the Ministry of Finance. Besides, there was the problem of poor coordination of debt matters, as reflected in the absence of a central location for information relating to all external borrowings.

Elsewhere, such a central location, called the Debt Management Unit, organizes and maintains the flow of information relating to government, parastatal, Central Bank of Nigeria and private borrowings, and has a comprehensive coverage of all external borrowings of all sectors of the economy. A good step in the above direction was, however, taken in 2000 when the government set up a Debt Management Office (DMO) for the country. Presumably, the DMO is now responsible for coordinating debt matters.

However, the DMO will have to work closely with the principal agencies involved in formulating borrowing policies, in contracting and paying, and in managing external debt obligations. These agencies are usually the Ministry of Finance, the Central Bank of Nigeria, the Ministry of National Planning, and parastatals. The DMO should have sufficient powers, status, and authority to discharge its functions, especially to enforce the reporting requirements and to implement debt policies. The terms of reference of the DMO should be widely circulated to all ministries, parastatals, and creditors.

The need to build adequate human capacity for debt management cannot be overemphasized. Management skills, knowledge, and relevant technology are at present far from adequate in Nigeria for effective debt management. As debt management has become a high-tech activity, operators within the system need to be exposed to training and re-training to acquire relevant expertise and skills.

A core of debt management specialists needs to be developed. On the one hand are technical experts with practical knowledge of loan instruments, who keep in touch with external financial markets, and are aware of the wide range of alternatives that are available to the country. On the other hand are economists who can design and use economic models that help analyze the balance of payments and debt-related flows.

In general, the training requirements of staff for managing and using Debt Recording and Management System (DRMS) can be broad, depending on the education and experience of staff. From experience, there is usually a high rate of turnover of DMO staff, so the training becomes almost an ongoing task. The most fundamental requirement is to train staff to interpret loan agreements relevant to the country's portfolio. Essentially, a DRMS requires a balance of skills—economics, accounting, statistics, computing, and administration—and training courses have to be tailored to meet the varying needs at different levels. For effective skills to be developed, it is necessary to allocate high quality human resources.

Another very worrisome aspect of the institutional arrangement for debt management relates to the weak capacity for negotiation for debt relief with external creditors. Nigeria and other debtor countries individually negotiate with the creditors through the Paris Club and London Club. Negotiations have become a permanent and tortuous feature of the debt problems of these countries, with repeated rescheduling with the Paris Club imposing very heavy administrative and financial costs on them.

The negotiations involving individual debtors and the creditor debt clubs are actually sham negotiations. This is because most debtor countries approach the Paris Club hat in hand begging, as it were, for rescheduling. The creditor countries dictate all the terms in a manner the debtors find rather humiliating. Indeed, Ani (1997a) describes negotiations with the Paris Club as rather cosmetic, since the factors that determine the debt relief to be granted are dictated, rather than negotiated.

It is hardly surprising that extracting meaningful concessions on debt relief from creditors has been difficult. This leads us to revisit the issue of effective collective action on the part of debtors. They need an institutional framework to bring about appropriate agreements among the parties concerned. Some form of the much talked about debtors' cartel is indispensable. It will enable debtors to forge a common front, which would improve their capacity to proffer credible options at negotiations with creditors.

But where certain known obstacles make collective action impossible, then the option of collective inaction may become appealing. For example, this entails the non-payment of debt service by a significant number of debtor nations, and the more the default trend persists, the greater will be the ultimate erosion in the bargaining power of creditors (Cohen 1989, p. 17).

References

Ahmed, M., and L. Summers. 1992. "A Tenth Anniversary Report on the Debt Crisis." *Finance and Development.* 29(3).

Ani, A. A. 1997a. "Debt Burden in Developing Countries: Options for Africa." Paper presented at the All Africa International Public Relations Professional Development Conference, Cairo, Egypt, November 19–21.

_____. 1997b. "Nigeria's Debt Profile: Problems and Challenges." Paper presented at the CBN Seminar on the Debt Problem and the Nigerian Economy, Abuja, October 28—29.

Cohen, B. J. 1989. "Developing-Country Debt: Middle Way." *Princeton Essays in International Finance. 173.* Princeton, N.J.: Princeton University.

Greene, J. H., and M. S. Khan. 1990. *The African Debt Crisis.* AERC Special Paper 3. Nairobi: Initiatives Publishers.

Holsen, J. A. 1987. "Managing External Debt." In Yin-Kann Wen and Elie Canetti, eds., *National Economic Policymaking: The Key Elements.* Washington, D.C: International Bank for Reconstruction and Development.

Hussain, I., and J. Underwood. 1991. "The Problem of Sub-Saharan Africa's Debt—and the Solutions." In I. Hussain and J. Underwood, eds., *African External Finance In the 1990s.* Washington, D.C.: World Bank.

Iremiren, T. A. 1997. "The Evolution and Management of Nigeria's External Debt: The Way Forward." Paper presented at the CBN Debt Management Departmental Seminar on the Debt Problem and the Nigerian Economy, Abuja, October 28–29.

Obadan, M. I. 1988. "Developments in Nigeria's External Debt." In A. O. Phillips and E. C. Ndekwu, eds., *Economic Policy and Development in Nigeria*. Ibadan: NISER.

_____. 1992. "External Loans and National Development: The Nigerian Experience." *Economic and Business Review* 2(1): 45 – 66.

_____. "The International Debt Problem." Paper presented at the 1990 Concluding Seminars of the Senior Executive Course No. 12, National Institute for Policy and Strategic Studies, Kuru, Jos, October 8.

_____. 2000a. "Towards Resolving Africa's External Debt Crisis: Strategies and Policies." Paper Presented at the ACDESS Millennium Symposium on Making Africa Face the Challenges of the 21st Century through Mobilization for the Implementation of the Continent's Development Paradigms, Ijebu-Ode, Nigeria, December 18–21

Obadan, M.I., and A. F. Odusola. 1999. "Savings, Investment and Growth Connections in Nigeria: Empirical Evidence and Policy Implications." *NCEMA Policy Analysis Series* 5(2):

Usman, I. 1995. "Issues of Debt Management Strategy for Africa." *CBN Debt Trends* 1(1):

Part 3:
Exiting the Debt Trap

9

Why Nigeria Needs Debt Cancellation Now

JEFFERY SACHS
Professor of Economics
Director, Center for International Development
Harvard University

It is actually somewhat incredible that in 2001 we are still debating the basic question of whether Nigeria's debts should be canceled. The answer is absolutely obvious. It has been so for a decade. It is especially obvious with the return of democracy, and with the leadership of President Obasanjo. The answer is yes.

There is no doubt economically, financially, or socially that Nigeria's debts need to be canceled. Sadly, however, all of the great brainpower that should be directed every day toward fighting illiteracy, the HIV/AIDS pandemic, and malaria is still being spent arguing and debating and struggling with the international creditors to finally put this debt question behind Nigeria.

First, there is no economic difference between Nigeria and the 22 countries that have already been approved for

Heavily Indebted Poor Country (HIPC) debt reduction. The idea that somehow Nigeria is in one category, and that these 22 countries that have received debt cancellation are in another category is perhaps not true. If the 22 countries that are receiving debt cancellation deserve it, then so does Nigeria, by every sensible measure.

Nigeria and the 22 HIPC approved countries have similarities. Let us start off with per capita gross national product. Is Nigeria too rich to be a HIPC country? Not at all. The average per capita income of the 22 HIPC countries is US$390 per year. But according to the same data of the World Bank, the average per capita income in Nigeria is US$300 per year. Thus, by using a strict definition, Nigeria is poorer than the countries that have already been approved for HIPC. If we measure the gross national product (GNP) per capita in so-called purchasing power terms, then the 22 countries that have been approved have an average purchasing power-adjusted GNP per capita of US$1,200 per person. In Nigeria, it is US$740 per person. From the standpoint of poverty, Nigeria should receive debt relief ahead of those other 22 countries, and not behind.

Consider social indicators, such as life expectancy. The average life expectancy at birth in the 22 HIPC countries is 52 years, tragically low compared to the life expectancy of high-income countries, which is now roughly 77 years. Where does Nigeria stand? Nigeria's life expectancy is 53 years, almost the same as in the 22 HIPC countries. In terms of social need, in terms of burden of disease, in terms of urgency of a poverty and social strategy, Nigeria is exactly where the other HIPC countries are. What about economic performance? Nigeria has been suffering even more than the 22 approved HIPC countries. If we were to look at the change of per capita income in real terms, between 1980 and 2000, on average for the 22 HIPC countries, there has been a decline of 0.3 of 1 percent of GNP each year between 1980 and 2000. In other words, poor countries are getting even poorer. But Nigeria's decline has been even more significant: 0.6 of 1 percent of GNP, on average, each year between 1980 and 2000.

Nigeria is a country crying out for debt cancellation. If we look at the burden of debt relative to gross national income, according to the *World Development Indicators 2001* of the World Bank, for the 22 HIPC countries debt relative to gross national income is 90 percent, and for Nigeria it is 91 percent, essentially the same heavy burden, and the reason for Nigeria to get the same treatment and the same common sense as the 22 HIPC countries.

So what is going on? Why is there this big philosophical argument about Nigeria? It is certainly not because of need. It is notable that at the beginning of the HIPC initiative in 1996, Nigeria was on the list, along with other countries. Then it was mysteriously taken off the list owing, perhaps, to political and bureaucratic games in Washington.

There may be two reasons why Nigeria was quietly removed from the list. One could be the Abacha regime. No one wanted to give debt reduction to the Abacha regime. The other reason is that Nigeria is a large country of 120 million people. Since it is so large, some of the European creditors and the United States may have gotten cold feet. If Nigeria were to get relief, then perhaps the thinking went that maybe Indonesia is going to ask for debt cancellation.

Perhaps we should just focus on one specific point. Nigeria needs debt cancellation. Its status is comparable to the rest of the HIPC countries, and it was once on the list and deserves to be on the list now. Thus, all the broad philosophical discussion, in our view, are just obfuscation of these very basic points. We have tried the other path for Nigeria for more than 15 years, and we know that it does not work. This is not the first time Nigeria's debt problem has come up. Nigeria's debts have been rescheduled comprehensively three times between 1986 and 1991, and then again in the first round International Monetary Fund agreement in 2000. There was a 1986 rescheduling. It failed. There was a 1989 rescheduling. It failed. There was a 1991 rescheduling. It failed. Now there has been the interim rescheduling of 2000, and it is just a stop gap until serious negotiations can begin on debt cancellation for this year.

The point is that if we have tried the simple postponement route, and the debt burden keeps growing, then we need to recognize that we are not doing the correct thing; that is, we need cancellation rather than postponement. Perhaps the international community already knows this and for some reason will not acknowledge this point publicly.

Second, there is what we shall call a mythology about Nigeria that is held by many observers in Europe and the United States, and that is the mythology of a rich country somehow stealing its own resources. Many in the international community equate oil with being rich, but as the statistics indicate, Nigeria is poorer than the average HIPC approved country. Perhaps there has been mismanagement of natural resources, and that the richer are richer and the poor are poorer, but that is not the fault of the people, and the people, themselves, are under this incredible debt burden.

To demonstrate, Nigeria produces about 2 million barrels of oil each day. The average world price as of 2001, was roughly US$25 per barrel. Average daily revenues, therefore, are US$25 a barrel times 2 million barrels per day, or US$50 million a day for Nigeria. But of course, foreign oil companies own part of that oil and there are costs of production. What is left over, net of the foreign income stream and net of the cost of production, is considerably less than US$50 million a day, perhaps US$30 million a day, which means $91.25 per Nigerian per year.

It is time to do something serious. Unfortunately, in our opinion, the creditors have not been serious. What distinguishes Nigeria from the other HIPC countries is that even though it is extremely impoverished and in need of resources, it is relatively easy to press on Nigeria for debt servicing, because the export revenues go into one basic pipeline, both literally and figuratively. There is a flow of money that is easy for creditors to grab, even if Nigeria desperately needs the money. So the creditors grab the money and squeeze an impoverished country. In doing so, they make it incredibly hard, in our opinion, to stabilize democracy and to get needed economic reforms underway.

In 1999, during a delicate moment of transition to democracy, the creditors got US$1.9 billion in actual debt service. In the year 2000, the creditors took US$1.5 billion from Nigeria in actual debt service. That, we know, was about three times the national education budget for a country with illiteracy rates of about 40 percent. .

Could this be the right priority? The US$1.5 billion

of debt service in 2000 was roughly nine times the public health budget for a country on the cusp of a massive HIV/AIDS pandemic, and suffering from pervasive malaria, tuberculosis, and other killer childhood diseases. Could it really be right to take nine times the public health budget?

The creditors do not understand the realities of poverty in Nigeria. The fact that it is easy to grab revenues out of Nigeria's oil pipeline is the ironic and sad part of this. Nigeria is a HIPC country like the rest. It needs debt cancellation. And yet it has still been pressed and forced to make significant debt payments.

There is one final myth that is extremely important to dispel, and that is the myth of a country that has no economic reform. There are many in the international community whose memory is so saturated with images of corruption that they cannot see through their myopia the real truth of Nigeria's struggling democracy and the new regime's desire to consolidate the rule of law, democracy, and economic reform.

If a broader view is taken—we can see the vast amount of progress that is occurring. The president has organized a national poverty eradication council and a series of initiatives aimed at poverty reduction. Universal basic education is a major initiative. A roll back malaria campaign has been started to try to get malaria under control. The government even hosted the first Africa-wide summit on malaria in Abuja, Nigeria, last year. There has been a major new effort to get HIV/AIDS under control, including a novel and brave pilot program to introduce antiretroviral therapy in Nigeria, something that the government is just now starting. There was a huge accumulation of foreign exchange reserves from the higher oil prices last year, proving that the country did not just profligately diffuse these oil revenues or put them into corruption, but prudently saved them.

Nigeria has already demonstrated that it can husband reserves and that it is not just a free-for-all as it seemed to be during many years of the Abacha regime. Big anti-corruption efforts are underway, even if they remain imperfect. But no one can doubt how significant a change has been in the past two years, in the new democracy, and how much more the rule of law can take hold if democracy is given a chance in Nigeria.

There is also real progress on privatization, including the auctioning of the lines for cellular telephony, and the proposed privatization of NITEL. These are substantial policy initiatives. From experience as an economic advisor all over the world to countries in extreme crisis, Nigeria is moving forward, despite the obstacles thrown up by the international community, and not because of the support but despite the obstacles.

Debating the general philosophy of debt reduction is all well and good in a vacuum, but there is real anguish out there. Dozens of countries need debt reduction to fight poverty, and Nigeria is one of them. By every standard it fits within the HIPC initiative. It is a shame that the rich countries have not said so clearly.

Second, there is a great political value to being clear that successful reform will lead Nigeria out of the debt trap. To have a clear incentive—one where the national assembly will properly understand that good policies will help get the country out of debt—will require the creditors to make a clear statement, rather than the obfuscating policies that have been common in recent years. Making such a clear statement has been inhibited by all sorts of mythology: the mythology of no reform, the mythology of the oil-rich country, the mythology that Nigeria is somehow different from the HIPC countries, even though Nigeria was a HIPC country once upon a time.

The creditors should make it clear that Nigeria will get deep debt cancellation as part of a process of fundamental economic and social reform. If Nigeria meets its commitments of effectual economic and social reform in the coming years, then it has proven itself worthy of debt cancellation. Economically, that means opening and privatizing the economy. In social policy it means strongly bolstering the education sector, both primary and university, as well as the health sector to fight HIV/AIDS, malaria, tuberculosis, diarrhea disease, and respiratory infection and all the other health problems a poor country has.

But the creditors must also live up to their side of the bargain and accept debt cancellation, because that is the bargain that will make Nigeria's democracy the lasting success it surely can be, and will make the Nigerian economic recovery the lasting success it surely can be.

10

International Experience of Aid and Debt Strategies:
Implications for Nigeria

PAUL COLLIER
Director, The World Bank

The democratic government of Nigeria faces enormous challenges. Nigeria has the potential for economic leadership on the African continent, but to realize this potential it has to overcome constraints from the past. One of these constraints is that the government has inherited nearly US$30 billion of indebtedness incurred by previous governments. It has inherited little else. The country is poorer than before it spent this US$30 billion. The US$30 billion is itself but a small part of the resources that previous governments have mismanaged. Nigeria has little to show for the US$280 billion of oil income that accrued over the same period. Whatever happened to those huge sums?

Until Nigerians face up to this past they will not become masters of their own future. Nigeria's economic past was characterized by two processes: waste and capital flight. So much of its capital went abroad that Nigerians now have even more foreign assets than they have foreign debts.

Prospects for Debt Relief

If Nigeria were to fully service its debt, given the way it is currently structured, then the cost in the coming year would be around US$5.3 billion. This is a large amount relative to the total debt of US$30 billion because so much of the debt is constituted by arrears rather than agreed borrowing. Quite reasonably, the Nigerian government did not want to pay US$5.3 billion service payments on a debt of US$30 billion. The strategy of General Abacha was unilaterally to impose a ceiling on actual repayments. However, this built up further arrears and worsened Nigeria's reputation.

It was thus, an expensive strategy. The alternative strategy, which the government has recently implemented, has been to reach an agreement with its creditors. There is a distinction between an agreement on rescheduling and an agreement on debt forgiveness. With rescheduling we agree on changing the time path of repayments and consolidate arrears, thus making them much less expensive. Through rescheduling Nigeria has been able to reduce service payments from US$5.3 billion to around US$2 billion.

There are obviously precedents for debt relief, notably the present initiative for a Highly Indebted Poor Country (HIPC). However, debt relief requires donors and the international financial institutions (IFI) to divert money from other uses. In effect, agencies will be asking themselves, "Why should we divert our budgets from other poor countries to Nigeria?" In practice, to be successful in gaining debt relief we need to demonstrate two conditions: that we have a good moral case and that we can use the money well.

Nigeria can probably demonstrate that it has a good moral case. Creditors might reasonably be asked to bear some of the responsibility for lending. Winning this argument is absolutely necessary for debt relief, because without a good moral case debt relief is a nonstarter. However, it is not sufficient. The campaigners for Jubilee 2000 and the governments and international agencies participating in HIPC were agreed that resources should only be diverted into debt relief if resources will be used effectively to reduce poverty.

In fact, this second condition of effective utilization of resources applies not just to debt relief, but also to aid more generally. This is important because Nigeria will probably find it easier to attract international public resources in the form of aid than in the form of debt relief. Whether the resources are labeled "debt relief" or "aid" is of little significance for the Nigerian economy. Politicians, both in Nigeria and in the creditor nations, might prefer one label or the other for this resource transfer, but labels are not the issue. What matters is the scale of the resource transfer.

At present, the scale of the resource transfer that donors and the international agencies are willing to provide to Nigeria is constrained by doubts about the ability to use the money effectively. As Nigerians know better than anyone else, over a long period, Nigerian governments demonstrated spectacular waste in public expenditure. This is the reason why it needs debt relief, and it is also the reason why at present creditors will be cautious.

Until Nigeria demonstrates good use of its large oil revenues, donors will be wary of diverting resources from poor countries, which do not benefit from such revenues. Donor budget decisions for the coming year have already been taken, and in very round numbers the likely flow of aid/debt relief resources to Nigeria will be about US$1 billion.

Starting from legal liabilities of US$5.3 billion, rescheduling has reduced payments to around US$2 billion, and the inflow of aid will further reduce net payments to around US$1 billion. In terms of the annual resource flow next year, this would be equivalent to having about 80 percent forgiven. Whether agencies choose to label it "forgiveness" or "rescheduling plus aid" is a matter of politics, and not of economics.

How can Nigeria improve on this outcome? Nigeria will need a strategy for the medium term. The heart of such a strategy will be to understand what determines donor and IFI decisions on resource allocation, and use that understanding to change their decisions. Those donors who are important for Nigeria, such as the U.K.'s Department for International Development (DFID), have clear criteria for the allocation of their resources. Indeed, these criteria are similar to those of the World Bank. The core purpose of both DFID and World Bank resources is to reduce poverty. Winning the case for debt relief depends upon allaying the fears that more resources would suffer the same fate as past resources, that is, waste and capital flight. These fears cannot be allayed overnight

Potentially, Nigeria can receive substantial aid/debt relief because it has such severe poverty. However, at present donor fears are not foolish. Nigeria has only a limited capacity to absorb aid effectively, partly because it has such a large oil income. Oil revenue accruing to the Nigerian federal and state governments is a foreign resource inflow analytically equivalent to aid. Whether the Nigerian government gets a check from the British government (aid) or British Petroleum (oil) really makes little difference to its effect upon growth.

We find that aid and other such foreign resources raise growth, but only up to a point. Each extra dollar yields less additional growth, and at some point another extra dollar yields no additional growth whatsoever. This is the *saturation point*. Donors are unlikely to provide sustained resource inflows that take the economy beyond the saturation point.

What determines the saturation point? It depends upon the policy and institutional environment. The better economic policies and institutions are, the more foreign resources the government can effectively use. This is not surprising. Good policies and institutions improve the investment climate and so make all investments, including public expenditure, more productive. This is just common sense, but modern economics can take us further because it can quantify. Within reason, we now know at what point the Nigerian government becomes saturated with foreign resources.

The World Bank assesses policies and institutions on a six-point scale, a score of 1 being really bad and of 6 being really good. Of course, in detail these assessments will always be a matter for debate, but globally higher scores have been associated with faster growth, so it is reasonable to believe that these scores reflect some underlying realities of differences between countries.

As a rule of thumb, the saturation point is around six times the policy score. Hence, with really bad policies (a score of 1) a country is saturated when foreign resources accruing to the government are around 6 percent of gross domestic product (GDP), while with really good policies it is saturated only when they reach around 3 percent of GDP. How good are Nigerian policies and institutions? Well, World Bank staff rate them as neither very bad, nor as very good, but they think that they are worse than average. Such an assessment does not seem to be very controversial. If Nigerian policy and institutional environment had been good then it would have had more to show for the oil revenue. If this assessment is broadly accepted, then Nigeria's saturation point is presently when foreign resources reach around 17 percent of GDP.

If Nigeria's saturation point for foreign resources accruing to the government is currently only around 1 percent of GDP, then we face a severe problem. Over the coming year Nigeria's oil income is projected at around US$16.9 billion. Its debt service net of the aid inflow will be around US$1 billion, so that the net foreign resource inflow would be around US$15.91 billion. This is around 40 percent of GDP, far in excess of the saturation point at which such resources are ineffective in the growth process.

That Nigeria has so little to show for its massive oil income and borrowings over the past 30 years is because its resource inflow has been around double its saturation point. Only a country with superb policies and institutions could have productively absorbed foreign resources accruing to the government as large as 4 percent of GDP. Given Nigeria's actual policies and institutions, while the first half of the resource inflow probably helped the economy, the other half probably harmed it.

How can excess resources harm an economy? One route is "Dutch disease": an inflow of foreign resources, which damages exports. Although the Dutch were the first to suffer this problem, Nigeria has become the foremost international example. Nigeria used to export huge amounts of cocoa and groundnuts, but these industries were destroyed during the oil boom. Another route by which excess foreign resources are harmful is corruption. An inflow of easy money unrelated to taxpayer effort is conducive to the emergence of narrow elites who fight among themselves to control the rents.

Such adverse effects of Nigeria's foreign resource inflows were avoidable. Had policy and institutions been better, the economy could productively have absorbed them. Better policies would have raised the growth rate of the non-oil economy, and this would have reduced the share of oil revenue relative to GDP. Imagine that a decade ago, instead of leading the economy to ruin General Abacha had led it to reform. To be concrete, imagine that he had introduced the sort of reforms that the government of Uganda actually implemented. Over the last decade the Nigerian non-oil economy has stagnated. If it had matched Uganda's, then it would have grown at 7 percent a year. Since Nigeria's economy has far more natural advantages than that of Uganda—a larger scale, a better location, a more educated population—to assume that with similar policies we would only have achieved the same performance is very conservative. Yet even with a 7 percent growth rate over the decade the non-oil economy would have doubled. This would have reduced the relative importance of oil in the economy. The oil revenue net of debt service would have come down from 40percent of GDP to 25 percent.

Not only would better policies have reduced the share of net oil revenue in GDP, it would have raised the capacity of the economy to absorb such revenues. Recall that as a rule of thumb, that an economy's saturation point is six times its policy score. If Nigeria had as good a policy environment as Uganda, then its saturation point for foreign resources would be much higher: not 17 percent but around 24 percent.

Now, bring these numbers together. With better policies over a decade the net oil inflow as a share of GDP would have fallen to around 25 percent, while the saturation point—the point at which further resources would be ineffective—would have risen to around 24 percent. In other words, the country would just have been able to absorb more. The Ugandan level of policies are not the gold standard but rather the threshold beyond which Nigeria can demonstrate that additional aid can be used effectively to supplement oil revenues. With its large population Nigeria can potentially attract more aid/debt relief than Uganda, but to do so it will need policies, which are better than current Ugandan policies.

Repatriating Nigeria's Foreign Assets

It is even more important for Nigeria to attract back its overseas assets than it is for it to get relief from its debts;

that is, its foreign assets are bigger than its foreign debts. During previous oil booms, as public investment rose, private investment fell. People were shifting their assets out of the country. Why did this happen? Most Nigerians believe that the reason for this capital flight was corruption. A corrupt elite embezzled the oil revenue and took it abroad for safekeeping. This is indeed part of the story. The right and proper response to this corruption has been to pursue the foreign bank accounts of those guilty of corruption. Nigeria has the right to total cooperation from foreign governments in this important venture. But it is only part of the story.

Surprisingly, the main driver of capital flight is not corruption. In countries with poor investment climates, people with honestly acquired savings lack domestic opportunities to invest it. Instead, they place their savings abroad. Most capital flight is like this: it is a portfolio strategy of the honest, rather than a concealment strategy by the corrupt. What does a poor investment climate mean in practice? Our research found two specific features were statistically important.

Where investors perceived that the environment was risky, capital flight was higher. We measured the perceived risk of the environment by the Institutional Investor Risk Ratings (IIRR). If the Nigerian government wants to attract back these overseas portfolios, then one good quantifiable objective is to improve this rating. It is published twice a year, in March and September, and is a rating by the investment community on a scale of 0 (total risk) to 100 (very safe). Know the score for Nigeria and determine to raise it step by step. Uganda has increased its score about five-fold over the past decade.

The other factor that was powerful in fueling capital flight was an overvalued exchange rate. The more overvalued the exchange rate, the larger is capital night. In the early 1980s there was a huge gap between the official and parallel exchange rates for the Naira. Nigeria hemorrhaged capital during this period. Currently, this gap has opened up again. Over the past 30 years an overvalued exchange rate has been the most consistent disaster in Nigerian economic policy. It has destroyed export industries and seduced wealth abroad.

But there are many factors that make for an improved investment climate. As we improve investment opportunities, people will repatriate their capital. This has happened elsewhere in Africa, and it will happen in Nigeria. It is obviously better for Nigeria to repatriate its own wealth than for it to rely upon foreign capital. But it will take laborious policy and institutional change, rather than exhortation.

Conclusion

Nigerians are rightly angry that the potential wealth of oil turned into the reality of debt. Huge oil resources still flow into the country These resources will go to waste, unless massive policy and institutional reform is undertaken. Nigerians are hoping that the World Bank and the donor community will reallocate resources to Nigeria. This is a worthy goal. However, the decisions of the World Bank and the donor community do not reflect patronage or preference. Rather, they reflect our goal of poverty-reducing growth. The scale of the debt forgiveness and aid that Nigeria receives will ultimately depend upon its own actions to improve its use of resources.

References

Bevan, David L., P. Collier and Jan W. Gunning. 1999. *The Political Economy of Poverty, Equity and Growth: Nigeria and Indonesia*. Oxford University Press.

Collier Paul, and David Dollar. 2001. *Aid Allocation and Poverty Reduction. European Economic Review*.

11
A Practical Strategy to Reduce Nigeria's Debt

MATTHEW MARTIN
Director, Debt Relief International

In the 1980s Nigeria's debt was an unsustainable burden, but few had faith that any debt relief provided would be spent for the benefit of Nigeria's people. Now we can say with confidence that Nigeria's new government is determined to use debt relief to foster economic growth and poverty reduction for the benefit of the Nigerian people.

In that context, we shall try here to present a practical strategy for reducing Nigeria's debt. What do we mean by "practical"? We have heard calls for the complete forgiveness of Nigeria's debt, and for the repudiation of odious debts contracted by previous regimes. We have also heard representatives of creditor institutions being somewhat cautious about their willingness to provide debt relief. Unfortunately for advocates of total debt cancellation, and also for those who do not want to provide debt relief to Nigeria, the international financial system works neither on the basis of morals nor entirely through power politics.

There are rules and precedents that should form an objective and practical basis for a strategy for reducing Nigeria's debt, which Nigeria's policymakers will then need to fight hard to implement. Our aim, based on experience of working with 34 African and Latin American countries, and of advising all the major international and donor organizations on debt relief issues, is to provide some guidance on such a strategy for Nigeria's policymakers and civil society.

The Rules of the Game

Nigeria owes approximately US$29 billion to its external creditors. Of this, nearly US$20 billion is owed to the Paris Club of creditor governments, more than US$2 billion to other governments, and more than US$3 billion each to multilateral financial institutions and to commercial creditors. It is clear that this debt "stock"—even after the relief provided to Nigeria last year—represents a major burden on Nigeria's economy—more than 70 percent of GDP, around 190 percent of exports and 150 percent of budget revenue. Similarly, the service on this debt will represent at least 20 percent of exports and budget revenue for the next few years.

The international community had established rules in the late 1990s, under the so-called Heavily Indebted Poor Countries' (HIPC) Debt Reduction Initiative, which allows debt relief to be provided on the basis of the per capita income level of the country and its debt burden. (Previously, debt relief was based on an annual or three-year financing need calculated by the International Monetary Fund (IMF) and on the amounts that creditors were prepared to provide.)

These depend on several factors.

- *The income level and lending category with the World Bank*

This is based on the World Bank's calculation (in consultation with the country) of its per capita income level, and the country's decision as to the terms on which it wishes to borrow in future.

If a country has an income level above US$785, it will be classified by the World Bank as a "blend" country. This means that it is eligible to borrow from the World Bank using a blend of International Bank for Reconstruction and Development (IBRD) (expensive) and International Development Association (IDA) (cheaper) resources. In this case, it cannot receive any cancellation of its debt. Its debt payments can only be postponed ("rescheduled") for a few years, using the Houston terms (between 3 and 10 years of grace period, followed by 10–15 years of payment).

If its per capita income is below US$785, it can apply for "IDA-only" status, which means that it will be able to borrow only from the IDA lending arm of the World Bank, and that it can have some of its debt canceled as a HIPC. The minimum amount of debt cancellation is now 67 percent.

- *The Sustainability of the country's debt*

This is measured by several ratios, which have been defined by the international community, though heavily criticized by many other sources for being inadequate to provide debt reduction, which will allow genuine growth, and poverty reduction in developing countries. (For the basis for these definitions and some of the criticisms, see Martin and Johnson (2000) and Johnson (2000)) These ratios are based on a somewhat obscure and much debated concept known as the present value (PV) of debt, which means the cost of paying the debt today (rather than in the future) as calculated by discounting the future debt payments by an interest rate that is supposed to represent the country's cost of borrowing (but does not).

The ratios defined by the international community indicate that if (after the minimum 67 percent debt reduction to which IDA-only countries are entitled) the PV of debt is below 150 percent of exports (the average of the last three years of exports) and 250 percent of budget revenue (for an unknown reason based on the last available year of revenue data), the country is entitled only to the minimum 67 percent debt reduction. Though independent analysts have suggested that the budget ratio is far too high, and that the crucial ratios have nothing to do with PV and should be based on debt service/budget revenue ratios, they have not prevailed in G7 discussions, which decide the ratios. If either of these ratios is higher than the threshold levels after the minimum 67 percent debt reduction, then the country can receive higher levels of debt cancellation up to 90 percent under the enhanced HIPC initiative.

• *The "track record" of the country in executing programs agreed with the IMF (standby programs for non-IDA only countries, and poverty reduction and*

A Practical Strategy to Reduce Nigeria's Debt

growth facility programs for IDA-only countries) This determines the timing of the debt relief that can be provided to a country. As shown in figure 1, in principle an IDA-only country can receive only 67 percent debt service cancellation for the first three years of the "track record."

Thereafter, at what is known as the "decision point," a country can receive a 67 percent reduction of its debt stock or, if its ratios exceed the levels described above, a 90 percent reduction of its service for the following few years. This will be followed by 90 percent debt stock reduction by non multilateral creditors (or more if necessary to get the debt down to the sustainability ratios discussed above) plus some reduction from the multilateral institutions, at what is known as the "completion point." However, in practice, during 2000 many countries have shortened both of these three year periods considerably, and receiving 90 percent service reduction after track records as short as 9–12 months and 90 percent stock reduction after a period as short as two years. In some cases this has been in recognition of a past track record before the HIPC initiative was designed. In several, however, a shortening of the first period has not reflected any consistent prior track record.

In addition, many creditor countries are prepared to provide 100 percent debt service cancellation from the decision point, and 100 percent debt stock cancellation from the completion point, for all HIPC countries, whether or not they have unsustainable ratios after 67 percent debt reduction.

THE DEBT TRAP IN NIGERIA

Figure 1. HIPC Initiative

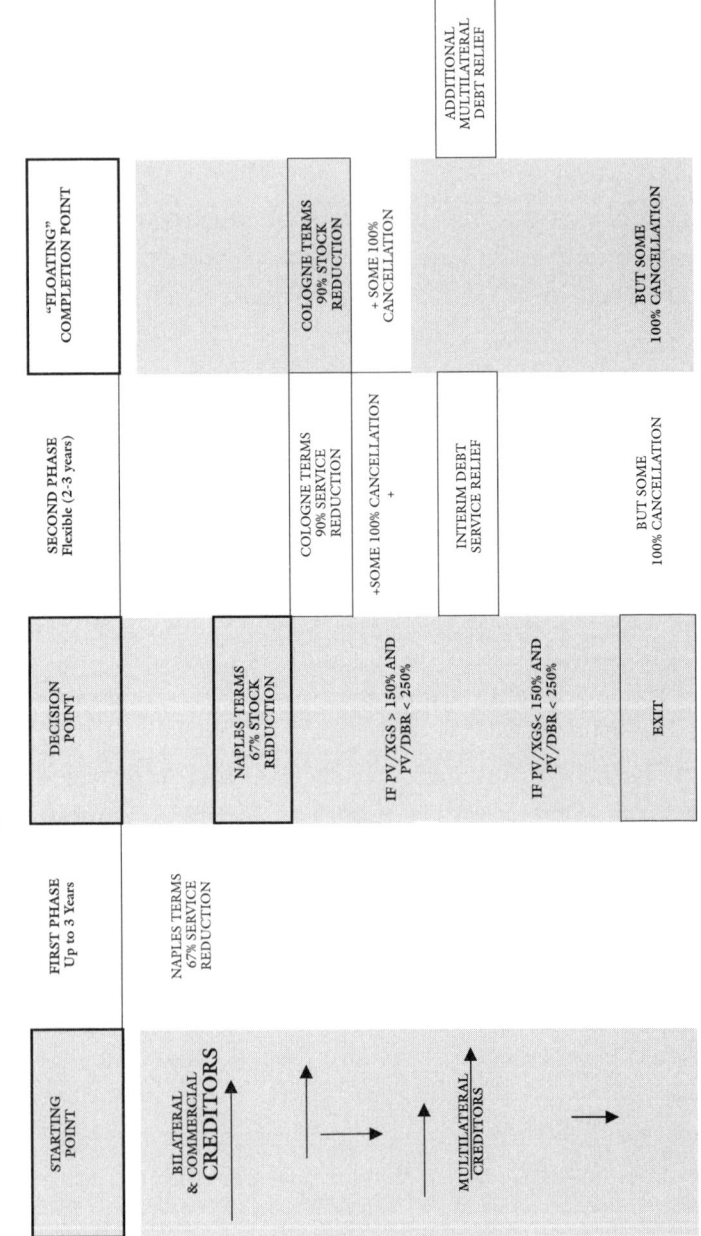

XGS/GDP > 30% and DBR/GDP > 15% must also be met
Debt Relief International, August 2000

Nigeria's Existing and Prospective Debt Relief

Existing Relief
It seems that the international community has not been particularly generous to Nigeria in the debt relief it has provided in the last few years. On December 13, 2000, Nigeria received from the Paris Club only a postponement of its debt service on Houston terms, with some service payable much more rapidly (over five years). This debt relief covered only payments falling due in 2000 and the first half of 2001, though additional clauses offered to extend it through the rest of 2001 if Nigeria continued to agree a program with the IMF. While Paris Club creditors offered to provide more relief in 2001, they did not say whether this would involve postponement (rescheduling), canceling service, or canceling stock.

Commercial creditors have also not provided any debt relief in 2000, because the Paris Club was prepared to accept that earlier debt relief was sufficient to be comparable with its current relief. Current negotiations indicate that commercial debt might be reduced by around 20 percent in present value terms, which would be much less than the relief available under HIPC (though more than the Paris Club is currently giving Nigeria).

There has been no discussion so far at a formal level of debt cancellation by multilateral creditors, and no information was available on whether non-Paris Club governments have provided any relief

Relief Prospects
The above treatment of Nigeria's debt has been justified by the fact that it is continuing to be a blend country. Yet,

according to its latest per capita gross domestic product (GDP) figures, Nigeria is well below the IDA-only threshold, and it has not borrowed from IBRD since 1993, because it has not been able to afford such loans. The international community has been relying on Nigeria's blend status to deny it any significant debt relief, above all because Nigeria owes such huge amounts of money to major G7 creditor governments that they do not wish to have to write off its debt; and because its borrowing needs would absorb a considerable portion of IDA resources if it were IDA-only.

There is no technical reason why Nigeria should not have IDA-only status at the World Bank. What is required is a political level campaign to ensure that G7 leaders are convinced that it should receive this status, of the type which Bosnia and Yugoslavia (countries with much higher per capita incomes than Nigeria) have recently conducted successfully. Were Nigeria to reach agreement with the World Bank that it should be IDA-only, it could immediately be entitled to a cancellation of 67 percent of its debt service and, after a certain track record of following IMF programs, to cancellation of 67 percent of its debt stock at the decision point.

In addition, commercial creditors would be obliged to provide terms, which were formally comparable to those of the Paris Club; that is, a 67 percent reduction as opposed to the only 20 percent reduction that is currently being negotiated, and which would represent a financial killing for creditors who have mostly written the debt off. Non-Paris Club government and commercial creditors would also be obliged to provide terms comparable with the Paris Club (67 percent reduction).

A Practical Strategy to Reduce Nigeria's Debt

Should Nigeria's ratios be "unsustainable" after such relief (which will depend mainly on the level of oil prices over the next few years), it could get 90 percent or more of debt service relief and some cancellation of its multilateral debt as well. Will this happen? A recent debt sustainability analysis conducted by the Nigerian government and the IMF indicated that, after a 67 percent reduction of the service due in the next three years, Nigeria's PV/export ratio would fall below the HIPC threshold of 150 percent by 2005, and on that basis declared Nigeria's debt to be sustainable, with two successive Paris Club flow reductions of 67 percent covering three years of debt service each, and a 20 percent PV stock reduction by commercial creditors.[1]

Of course, whether or not Nigeria's debt is unsustainable after a 67 percent debt stock reduction, it would still be eligible as a HIPC for 100 percent debt cancellation from some major G7 creditor governments, notably the United Kingdom, Germany, and the United States, which together account for around US$10 billion of its debt. In other words, just by being declared a HIPC country (even if it was then not eligible for full HIPC relief), Nigeria could receive around US$20 billion of debt relief.[2]

When would this relief be available? The 67 percent service reduction should be able to begin immediately after the agreement on IDA-only status.[3] If Nigeria stays on track with its poverty reduction programs endorsed by the international community, then the decision point (at which it would receive 67 percent stock treatment, plus 100 percent cancellation of service by some creditors, or if eligible the 90 percent service treatment) would come by (latest) the middle of 2004, if not earlier. Finally, the completion point at which it would get 100 percent cancellation of debt stock from some G7 countries, and if eligible for HIPC relief, 90 percent stock reduction from the Paris Club and other commercial and government creditors, would come by 2007. So the vast bulk of this US$20 billion would come within the next 6 years.

What would this mean in terms of savings for the budget to spend on poverty reduction? Owing to the way in which different creditors deliver their relief, annual service savings tend to be around 10 to 15 percent of the headline amount for the first few years. This would mean savings of around US$1 to 2 billion a year, compared to paying all debt service on schedule. However, this is only a preliminary estimate, and Nigerian staff will need to do their own more comprehensive "debt sustainability analysis," testing loan by loan the impact of receiving HIPC status, for us to identify the net benefits of HIPC compared to existing debt relief strategies.[4]

In other words, were Nigeria to be declared IDA-only and included in the list of potential HIPCs—and even if its debt was sustainable after 67 percent stock reduction—it could receive four times as much debt relief as has been assumed in the recent DSA (US$20 billion instead of US$5 billion), and around US$1 to 2 billion a year in debt service savings to spend on development and poverty reduction.

Commonly Asked Questions

Will not going for HIPC mean sacrificing Nigeria's economic policy independence?

As the international rules currently work—even if many of us would rather it were otherwise—countries have to agree on an economic reform program (or if they are IDA, only a poverty reduction strategy) endorsed by the IMF and World Bank before they can receive any relief. Nigeria received its relief from the Paris Club last year only on the basis of a standby agreement with the IMF (even though it is not borrowing the money from the IMF, it is following policies agreed with it).

Going for IDA-only and HIPC status would not add extra conditions to the current program. But it would change the process and the content of the conditions considerably. Standby agreements in most countries are reached through behind-the-scenes negotiations between government officials and the IMF and World Bank, and which are often not led by the government officials. They contain little or no analysis of the effects of the proposed economic policies on long-term poverty reduction.

In contrast, the Poverty Reduction Strategies (PRSs) agreed for IDA-only borrowers have been more transparent, generally resulting from a process of consultation with civil society in the country. In many cases, the lead for PRSs is undertaken more by the country than traditional standbys, and much more oriented to reducing poverty both through faster growth and through direct government action. Initial PRSs have rightly been criticized in many countries for not allowing enough participation by civil society, leadership by government, or analysis of the effects of policies on poverty reduction, but nobody would disagree that in all of these respects they are an improvement on traditional standby agreements. Given the Nigerian government's commitment to transparent and participative design of economic policy, to leading the dialogue with the international institutions, and to reducing poverty, the PRS process will involve much less sacrifice of government and national priorities.

Of course, some may advocate alternative policy routes involving no agreement with the international institutions and growing out of or defaulting on debt, or changing the international financial system to remove the link between conditionality and debt relief. Nigeria and its people can analyze the costs and benefits of the former, and the likelihood of the latter.

Will not HIPC status ruin Nigeria's creditworthiness for new development finance?
In other countries that have applied for HIPC status there has often been strong initial concern in some quarters that this involves, first, sacrificing national pride by publicly declaring the country to be heavily indebted and poor and, second, and more importantly, sacrificing access to new development finance. The first is true, but the second is not.

Nigeria has access to five potential types of development financing (starting with the most expensive):

- Commercial lending to the private sector
- Commercial lending to the government or parastatals
- Export credit or other slightly subsidized lending (for example, the IBRD, IMF standby) to the government or parastatals
- Aid loans and grants
- Non-debt creating finance; that is, foreign direct

investment or portfolio investment.

Commercial lenders take their decisions on the basis of the likelihood of repayment by the borrower. In the case of countries with substantial debt burdens and arrears, they often insist on guarantees of repayment (for example, by consignments of oil exports or other guaranteed earnings from government or a parastatal, or by a guarantee from the headquarters of a multinational corporation or another reputable agency such as international financial corporations for the private sector). The effect of substantial debt relief can only be to improve the country's prospects of payment by reducing the debt overhang and future service burdens, and to clear existing arrears. As a result, HIPCs and non-HIPCs have both felt positive effects on new commercial financing (especially reducing borrowing costs for the private sector, and having major positive effects on FDI, international guarantees, and domestic private investment) from receiving substantial amounts of debt relief. In Nigeria's case it seems important to mention that these benefits mostly disappear when relief is only a small proportion of total debt (as is currently the scenario with a reduction of US$5 billion outside HIPC).

Export credit agencies and international institutions take their decisions to guarantee or cofinance commercial loans, or to lend directly, on roughly the same basis as commercial lenders (sometimes with slightly more complex systems for calculating country creditworthiness). When a country is in any significant arrears they tend to refuse to commit new loans, and sometimes to disburse existing ones. Their reaction to rescheduling—whether they restart lending—depends on whether they believe the debt relief provided is a credible treatment of the debt burden, and will allow the country to pay its debts in future, though some export credit agencies will lend even if this is not the case because they are so anxious to promote their own country's exports.

A larger reduction of the debt burden clearly provides more assurance to these lenders as well. Though many export credit agencies will indicate that more debt relief might reduce their willingness to lend in future, this has not been the case where countries have profitable projects, which need export credit loans.

Aid donors are increasingly focusing their financing on governments committed to poverty reduction. As was discussed, the PRS under IDA-only status are much more oriented in this direction, and can assist in mobilizing additional aid. The only countries whose aid or mixed credit loans might be negatively affected by going for debt relief are France and Japan, and they can usually be convinced to replace the loans with grants, or other donors can find cheaper money to replace them.

The main benefit of clearing the existing debt overhang, service and arrears is likely to be in improved prospects for non debt creating flows such as FD1 and portfolio investment. Nigeria is undoubtedly committed to not falling into the debt trap again, so this type of money (as well as the cheaper forms of lending such as aid and money from the international financial institutions) is much to be preferred to commercial and export credit loans.

Nigeria also needs to think carefully about the quality of the money it receives. Export credits tied to exports of an individual country have often sharply reduced the value for money of the associated loans, and lenders prepared to lend when a country has a very high debt overhang are often those that want to overprice their goods, or put much of the money in their own bank accounts up front (as well as a little into Nigerian overseas accounts). In the context of the Nigerian government's commitment to fighting corruption and increasing value for money in government procurement, the more debt relief Nigeria receives, the more transparent sources of funds are likely to increase.

Finally, debt relief itself should free substantial resources in the budget to spend more flexibly on promoting development and fighting poverty in Nigeria and on priority areas such as education, health, water and sanitation, rural roads, and electricity, and do it in a much more flexible way without all the project-by-project conditions that normally delay disbursement of new funds.

Overall, there is no doubt that Nigeria would make substantial net gains from getting more debt relief. It would be well worth the small sacrifice of national pride to recognize the fact that Nigeria is objectively both heavily indebted and poor, and thereby allow debt relief to help unlock the immense wealth of its natural resources and the skills of its people. The HIPC initiative is by no means perfect, but it is a lot better than what Nigeria is getting now.

Priorities for Immediate Action

These conclusions lead us to identify four priorities for immediate action:

- Conduct a full debt sustainability analysis (in a workshop run by Nigerian government staff from the Debt Management Office and other agencies concerned with macro forecasts and poverty reduction, assisted by the best international expertise) to assess the benefits of various types of debt relief in more detail
- Begin immediate discussions with the G7, IMF, and the World Bank for a declaration of IDA-only status by the time of completing successfully the current standby agreement with the IMF. Based on that declaration, negotiate to receive 67 percent debt service reduction from the Paris Club with a promise of stock treatment within two to three years, and similar terms from commercial creditors
- Based on that declaration, negotiate to receive 67 percent debt service reduction form the Paris Club with a promise of stock treatment within two to three years, and similar terms form commercial creditors
- Begin the design of a national poverty reduction and growth strategy to absorb the savings from debt relief.

Notes

1. This analysis was conducted before the Debt Management Office database has been completed, and therefore on the basis of an average discount rate without any loan-by-loan analysis. As such its results should be treated with extreme caution, as experience from other countries demonstrates that such analysis can have margins of error of up to 25 percent compared to detailed loan-by-loan analysis.
2. It has not been possible to translate PV reduction into nominal stock reduction pending the debt stock analysis, though they would be the same in the case of any 100 percent cancellations and any other creditors agreeing to cancel 67 percent of debt up front (rather than reducing interest rates). This is made up of around US$16.6 billion in nominal stock from the Paris Club (100 percent write off by Germany, the United Kingdom, and the United States and 67 percent by other creditors), US$2.2 billion from commercial creditors, and US$1.5 billion from non-Paris Club creditors.
3. In addition, if the United Kingdom were to extend its decision of December 2000 to Nigeria, all debt service due to the United Kingdom after the 67 percent reduction would be set aside into a trust fund to be released at the decision point for Nigeria to spend on poverty reduction.
4. Debt Relief International, a non-profit organization funded by the governments of Austria, Denmark, Sweden, Switzerland, and the United Kingdom, has assisted more than 35 countries over the last six years in building their own capacity to conduct such analysis

(rather than doing the analysis for them through expensive consultants or advisors). It is already conducting an extensive program of capacity building in virtually all the Anglophone countries of West Africa, in cooperation with the West African Institute for Financial and Economic Management, an institute run and owned by the central banks of Anglophone West African states. A Nigerian delegation led by Mansur Muhtar participated in a regional workshop on designing strategies to negotiate external debt reduction, at which many of the issues raised in this chapter were analysed and discussed. (See Martin and Aguilar: 2001)

References

Johnson, Alison. *The Fiscal Sustainability of Debt.* Available from www.dri.org.uk.
Martin, Matthew. 1991. *The Crumbling Façade of Africa's Debt Negotiations.* New York: Macmillan.
Martin, Matthew, and Juan-Carlos Aguilar. 2001. *The HIPC Debt Strategy and Analysis Capacity-Building Program.* Available from www.dri.org.uk.
Martin, Matthew, and Alison Johnson. 2000. *Implementing the HIPC Initiative: Key Issues for HIPC Governments.* Available from www.dri.org.uk,
Martin, Matthew, and Michel Vaugeois. 1999. "Changing the HIPC Ratios." Report. Department of International Development, London.
Martin, Matthew, and Juan-Carlos Vilanova. 1999. The Paris Club: *A Guide for Debtor Countries.* Available from www.dri.org.uk.

12
A Global Agenda for Dealing with Debt

ANN PETTIFOR
Coordinator, Jubilee 2000 Plus

In developing countries, billions in reserves have been bled out of central banks, billions in asset values have been destroyed, and millions of workers have fallen into poverty and chronic insecurity. Global capital markets have acted as gigantic engines of inequality, transferring wealth from the weak to the strong, from debtors to creditors, wage earners and taxpayers to the holders of paper claims, from productive to financial activity.
—Levitt (1999)

We live in a global economy once again dominated, as in the 1920s, by international finance capital. According to one estimate, before 1970, 90 percent of all international transactions were accounted for by trade, and only 10 percent by capital flows. Today, despite a vast increase in global trade, that ratio has been reversed, with 90 percent of transactions accounted for by financial flows not directly related to trade in goods and services (see Kelly 1998.)

Most of these flows have taken the form of highly volatile stocks and bonds, investment and short-term loans. By 1992, financial assets from the advanced nations of the Organization for Economic Cooperation and Development (OECD) totaled $35 trillion—twice the economic output of the OECD. McKinsey and Company believe that the total financial stock will have reached $53 trillion by the year 2000, "triple the economic output of the OECD economies." (Greider 1997, p. 232)

These changes to the global economy—the shift from the dominance of industrial capital to finance capital—did not come about naturally or spontaneously. They are the result of deliberate policymaking, driven first by the city of London and the British government, and later by Wall Street and the U.S. government. Both governments use the International Monetary Fund (IMF) as an agent for implementation of effectively deflationary policies, whose ultimate purpose is not, as they have recently taken to insisting, to reduce poverty but to protect the value of creditor assets.

In the 1920s, similar deflationary economic policies were applied to justify the dismissal of public servants, to suppress wages, and to maintain unemployment. The most important of these policies was the stabilization of currencies, fixed in terms of gold, to guarantee debt service to foreign bondholders. Much the same happens today. Instead of the gold standard we have "dollarization." Currencies are once again stabilized to guarantee debt service to foreign bondholders and other creditors. The IMF, agent of all international creditors public and private, intervenes in the market and imposes and encourages a range of policies, including dollarization, currency boards, and fixed exchange rates, whose real purpose is to defend the value of the assets of international creditors and lenders.

Central to our planned global economy dominated by finance capital is the powerful lever of debt. Debt acts as the key mechanism for the transfer of wealth from weak to strong, from debtor nations to international creditors, from taxpayers and wage earners to the holders of paper claims and from productive to financial activity. (Levitt 1999). Without the leverage of debt, IMF policymakers would not be able to impose policy changes necessary to ensure such transfers.

Nigeria's Odious, Phantom, and Unpayable Debts

Speaking at a joint press conference with president Olusegun Obasanjo during his visit to the country in October, 1999, President Clinton said, "It is neither morally right, nor economically sound, to say that young democracies like Nigeria, as they overcome the painful legacy of dictatorship or misrule, must choose between making interest payments on their debt and investing in the health and education of their children." (Abuja, October 28, 1999).

At another meeting with Kwesi Owusu, head of Jubilee 2000 Africa Initiative in March 2000, president Obasanjo averred that, "the time for an international commitment of deep debt reduction and forgiveness is now. Our foreign debt stands at U$31 billion, and continues to rise, not because of any significant additional borrowing, but mainly as a result of the cost of servicing what was actually borrowed in the past. In these circumstances, it is simply not possible to speak of any significant measure of development, for as long as we are obliged to allocate so much of our lean resources to debt servicing. It is morally unjustifiable for the poor people of Nigeria to suffer any longer." (Abuja, March 21, 2000)

Nigeria owes $30.3 billion, according to the World Bank's data for 1998. However, accounting of the debt was very poor during the Abacha years, and the debt may well be nearer to US$35 billion. About two thirds of the debt is to the Paris Club, with Britain, Germany, Japan, and France the largest creditors. More than US$15 billion of the debt to the Paris Club is in arrears. Nigeria, in recent years has made serious efforts to pay its commercial creditors and received rescheduling in 1992, but it effectively broke off working relationships with Paris Club creditors, and hence the large rise in arrears. The total figure (in 2000) owed to bilateral creditors is estimated at nearer US$22.5 billion.

Nigeria paid creditors a total of US$1.5 billion on average each year in the financial years 1998 to 1999 and 1999 to 2000. Of this about US$600 million was to the multilaterals, and US$250 million to private creditors. Payments to the Paris Club made up the remainder. The small arrears that existed with the multilaterals have been cleared, but arrears continue to mount with other creditors. By 2000 the IMF and the Paris Club were insisting that Nigeria devote US$3.6 billion—nearly 9 percent of the gross domestic product (GDP)—to debt service to Paris Club and the IMF, the World Bank, and regional bank creditors. The government made public its intention to use the gains from oil revenues for poverty alleviation, and allocated US$1.5 billion in the 2000 budget for external debt repayment.

The sums to be diverted by Nigeria to western creditors contrasts with resources available for poverty reduction. The new Poverty Alleviation Program passed by the National Assembly amounts to US$100 million, 0.3 percent of GDP. Health spending by the federal government is set at US$150 million, 0.4 percent of GDP. Education spending has been fixed at US$400 million, 1 percent of GDP. Despite the fact that Nigeria will not pay US$3.6 billion in debt service, creditors are still demanding 15 times in debt service what the Nigerian government is able to pay in poverty reduction. Having lent money to military dictators, and having failed to collect debts from those dictatorships, they are now coercing the new democratic regime into repayment of those odious debts.

Oil prices have risen from an average of US$18 in 1999 to a forecast US$29 in 2000. Oil and gas (the price of which is linked to oil) account for more than 90 percent of Nigeria's exports, and so the increase will mean significantly increased export earnings for this year. Exports in 1999 were US$13 billion and for 2000 will be about US$22 billion. This will result in a windfall of between US$5 and US$7 billion in government revenue. In June 2000, the managing director of the Nigerian National Petroleum Corporation (NNPC) announced that US$2 billion of arrears to the oil multinationals have been repaid, but this still leaves a further US$1 billion still to be settled.

We in the Jubilee 2000 movement believe that the case for using the windfall for poverty reduction, rather than for paying bilateral creditors, is overwhelming. Paris Club creditors are almost all enjoying unprecedented economic prosperity as a result of the long boom in industrialized countries. The poverty indicators in Nigeria are shockingly low, and on current trends Nigeria will not meet the 2015 development targets agreed to by members of the Development Assistance Committee of the OECD.

Nigeria short-changed by rich creditors

Nigeria is not in the Heavily Indebted Poor Countries (HIPC) initiative, not because it was not eligible but because creditors deemed it too costly to write off her debts. Because creditors act as witness, judge, and jury in the court of international debt, ruling on their own claims, the people of Nigeria have not been relieved of the phantom, and often odious, debts that hang like a millstone around their necks.

Nigeria was one of the original HIPC countries, defined by the World Bank and the IMF, as eligible for substantial relief. It was, quietly and mysteriously, dropped from the HIPC list in 1998. The reason given by the IMF was spurious: that Nigeria is eligible for nonconcessional loans from the International Bank for Reconstruction and Development (IBRD) as well as concessional loans from the soft-lending arm of the World Bank, the International Development Association (IDA). In other words that Nigeria was a "blend" country. But this was true for Nigeria when it was included in the HIPC list in the first place. Nothing had changed except the advent of democracy.

While it is true that Nigeria has outstanding debts to the IBRD as well as IDA, that is also true of 22 other HIPC countries. The Nigerian government was not aware that borrowing from the IBRD was likely to exclude it from eligibility for HIPC. The new democratic government has no intention of borrowing from the IBRD, and indeed its IMF agreement would prohibit it from borrowing from IBRD. So, in reality, the new government is taking Nigeria back to IDA-only status, which should make Nigeria eligible for HIPC debt relief.

Nigeria and the HIPC Sustainability Criteria

Debt is about 75 percent of Nigeria's GDP, very high in absolute terms. However, the IMF and the World Bank do not base eligibility on debt to GDP ratios. For the IMF, the key ratio is the debt to export ratio. Nigeria's ratios are dependent on volatile and fluctuating oil prices. Oil prices have been at less than US$20 a barrel over the last decade, but have moved up to US$30. Based on prices of around US$25 per barrel, Nigeria's oil export revenues (95 percent of all revenues) are of the order of US$18.3 billion.

Allowing for production costs and the share that goes to foreign firms, oil revenues would provide export earnings of no more than US$14.5 billion to Nigeria. This means that the effective debt to export ratio is more than 200 percent. The debt service due (US$3.6 billion) ratio to export revenues is 25 percent. Both these ratios exceed by far the ratios for eligibility for HIPC set by the IMF and the World Bank. The IMF and World Bank have never defended their decision to remove Nigeria from the HIPC list, despite repeated challenges for justification by Jubilee 2000 and other advocates.

Nigeria's Looted Wealth

As a result of capital flight and corruption, large amounts of Nigerian reserves are deposited in foreign banks and institutions. General Abacha alone deposited almost US$4 billion in western banks. This was clearly known to western bankers and creditors in London, Washington, Frankfurt, and Zurich. Lawyers acting for the new government are preparing to freeze US$500 million held in accounts in Britain and have warned the banks involved that they will face prosecution if they allow the money to leave the country before criminal proceedings are brought in British courts. US$1.2 billion has been frozen in banks in Switzerland and Luxembourg, but Britain is believed to have been the focal point of transactions that spanned more than 100 accounts in several countries. On the basis of a list of more than 500 transactions, most of the funds are thought to be in branches of the Midland (now HSBC), Barclays, Citibank, and the French Bank Credit Agricole-Indosuez. Mohammed Abacha, eldest surviving son of the late dictator, has been charged with corruption and money laundering as part of a Swiss investigation.

Nigeria and the DAC targets for 2015

Nigeria could only hope to reach the Development Assistant Committee (DAC) targets with complete debt cancellation and increases in aid flows. Nigerian GDP per capita is US$300 per person. Health spending per capita is a shocking US$1.5 per person. Life expectancy is 53 and falling because of HIV/AIDS; only 38 percent of children were immunized against measles from 1995 to 1997; 36 percent of under 5 children are underweight, and 51 percent of the population does not have access to safe water. In short, Nigeria is one of the poorest countries in the world.

Per capita income showed no increase between the years 1965 and 1998, a generation lost to progress. The country is ethnically divided, and collapsed social services combined with widespread disease, a spiraling HIV/AIDS epidemic, low life expectancy, high malnutrition, and low school attendance. Without substantial debt cancellation—not *rescheduling*—Nigeria will not meet the 2015 Millennium Development Goals.

Jubilee 2000 calculates that the difference between Nigeria's taxing capacity and its required social spending to meet the DAC targets is more than US$5 billion a year. This is more than its debt service due. Therefore, even if Nigeria's debt is entirely written off, it will still need additional aid of more than USUS$1 billion a year if it is to meet the internationally agreed poverty reduction targets for 2015. This means Nigeria needs total debt cancellation plus additional aid.

However, there is no sign that rich, powerful western creditors are going to relinquish their grip over the poorest people of Nigeria. They continue to demand that Nigeria's precious, scarce resources are transferred from the poorest to much richer financial institutions in western creditor nations.

Finance Capital, Human Rights, and Ethics

In the West concern about the injustice of international

financial relationships and by the domination of creditors, investors, and speculators over poor countries has been growing, amplified by the international Jubilee 2000 movement. The campaign's guiding principles were grounded in Judaic and Christian biblical ethics on human rights, opposition to usury, and the need for periodic correction to imbalances; that is, the Sabbath and Jubilee principles. The campaign drew on what Ched Myers called the "Hebrew Bible's vision of Sabbath economics, (which) contends that a theology of abundant grace and a communal ethic of redistribution is the only way out of our slavery to the debt system, with its theology of meritocracy and private ethic of wealth concentration" (*Sojourners Magazine*, 1998). These principles and ethics have, in turn, resonated with Muslims and others.

The link between debt bondage and ethics—as an issue of public as well as private morality—is, of course, ancient. Laws throughout history have been promulgated against usury. In England a series of post-reformation usury laws set maximum rates of legal interest for money lending that in 1713 finally settled at 5 percent. The limitation on interest was to remain operative throughout the early industrial period, and was finally abandoned only in 1854 (Cornish and Clark, 1989). A loan that fell foul of the usury law was unlawful and unenforceable by the lender.

Adam Smith in *Wealth of Nations* did not consider that free market notions justified the lifting of this "prudent fetter on cupidity." (*Wealth of Nations*, 1976 ed., pp. 356-358). Until quite recently it was possible for usurers to be excommunicated by the Catholic church, and usury is still a crime that can be fiercely punished under Islamic Sharia law. Attempts over the centuries to legislate against usury reflect ethical concerns about the exploitation of weak and vulnerable debtors by the collective actions of much richer, more powerful creditors.

Creditors have, throughout history, resisted such ethical "fetters on cupidity." As recently as March 2001, the U.S. Senate voted overwhelmingly for a measure that would make it harder for ordinary U.S. debtors to have their credit card and other unsecured debts erased under Chapter 7 of the U.S. bankruptcy code (*New York Times*, March 16, 2001). The Bush administration is promoting this measure as a result of effective bribery by the MBNA Corporation of Delaware, "the largest independent credit card issuer in the world," which as, the Republican campaign's biggest corporate donor, gave US$26 million during the 1997 to 2000 election cycle.

In condemning the Senate vote, the *New York Times* notes that "there is scant evidence that bankruptcy abuse is rampant. Studies consistently show that those obtaining Chapter 7 protection are truly in dire straits. That is partly because the credit card industry frequently bombards even low-income Americans who have a checkered credit history with offers for high interest loans. Now credit card issuers want the government to reduce all risk from their profitable business." (*New York Times*, March 16, 2001)

Fair, Countable, and Open Treatment

Adam Smith in *Wealth of Nations* asserted that "when it becomes necessary for a state to declare itself bankrupt, in the same manner as when it becomes necessary for an individual to do so, a fair, open, and avowed bankruptcy is always the measure which is both least dishonorable to the debtor, and least hurtful to the creditor." (*Wealth of Nations*, p 358). There is little that is fair and open about procedures to renegotiate the debts of poor countries like Nigeria today. For years the secretive Paris Club—a cartel of sovereign creditors—has dominated debt-rescheduling processes, hand-in-hand with the closed and bureaucratic IMF.

The Paris Club began life in 1956 to consider Argentina's external debt. It is an informal body representing all official and private creditors, including all OECD governments, the IMF, World Bank, and other multilaterals. It has no legal status, yet it has tremendous power over poor country debtors. In the words of a former secretary, M. De Fontaine Vive, as reported in *Euromoney*, September 2000, "the Paris Club is not an institution, it's a non institution. There is no charter and there is no manual." However, there are unwritten rules, and the most important of these is that the IMF and World Bank as official creditors are "preferred creditors"; that is, they must always be paid, above and before other creditors (individual government, bilateral and private creditors).

In other words, creditors are treated unequally by this "non institution." According to a recent report in *Euromoney*, Paris Club members "sit in a windowless conference hall while poor country debtors are crammed into a tiny meeting room downstairs. While the G7 creditors are treated to a grand lunch, the debtors are reduced to pleading with an official to order them pizza." Debtors are so badly prepared that they are beaten almost before they start. One of the creditors describes the experience as "humiliating and colonial."

Today, Professor Kunibert Raffer of the University of Vienna, Professor Jeffrey Sachs of Harvard, and Oscar Ugarteche, former professor of international finance at the Catholic University of Peru, are in the forefront of calls for an open, fair international insolvency procedure for sovereign states. Ugarteche reminds us of the history of state insolvency, and in particular the record of western nations in both writing off politically inconvenient debts, and, in the case of Britain's World War I debts, effectively repudiating their own debts to other nations (Ugarteche 2000).

Raffer points out that "under any insolvency procedure ... human rights and human dignity of debtors are given priority over unconditional repayment." He argues that "debtor protection is one of the two essential features of insolvency. The other is the most fundamental principle of the Rule of Law; that one must not be judge in one's own cause; like all legal procedures insolvency must comply with the minimal demand that creditors must not decide on their own claims" (Raffer 1999).

Raffer (1999) notes that "insolvency relief is not an act of mercy, but of justice and economic reason." The Bretton Woods Institutions (BWIs) he argues, "take decisions, but refuse to participate in the risks involved." He demonstrates that decision making by the BWIs "is not only delinked from financial responsibilities, their errors may even cause financial gains." This, Raffer asserts, is a system absurdly at odds with the western market system:

> At a time when riskless decision making by bureaucrats is abolished in the East, there is no reason why it should be preserved in the West. It is the most

basic precondition for the functioning of the market mechanism that economic decisions must be accompanied by (co)responsibility: whoever takes economic decisions must also carry financial risks.

If this link is severed—as it was in the Centrally Planned Economies of the former East efficiency is severely disturbed. The striking contrast between free-market recommendations given by the BWIs and their own protection from market forces must be abolished. (Raffer 1992)

Professor Jeffrey Sachs calls for an international standstill mechanism that would provide debtor-in-possession financing and a comprehensive and timely workout of the debts. Sachs notes the parallels between Macy's in New York and Russia in 1992, both of which went bankrupt in the same month (January 1992). Macy's filed for protection from creditors under Chapter 11. Russia had no protection from her creditors, and on the contrary her creditors moved in and took over "the shop." Macy's received an immediate standstill on debt servicing, and within three weeks of filing for bankruptcy was able to arrange a new loan of US$600 million from several New York commercial banks as part of court-supervised, debtor-in-possession financing.

Russia had no such luck! There was no standstill, and the Russian government had to wait over a year to receive from the IMF and World Bank as much money as Macy's had been able to borrow in three weeks. As a result the Russian government was politically weakened. By the time financing was arranged, many leading reformers had been ousted and Russia's stabilization program thrown off track.

Independent Arbitration

Raffer's call for a system of independent arbitration between sovereign debtors and their international creditors—widely amplified by the Jubilee 2000 movement—has recently been supported by the Secretary-General of the United Nations, Kofi Annan, who in September 2000 submitted a report to the General Assembly calling for "an objective and comprehensive assessment by an independent panel of experts not unduly influenced by creditor interests, while the existing processes are under way." Such an assessment, Annan argues, should not be restricted to HIPC countries, but should also encompass other debt-distressed low-income and middle-income countries.

It should include debt sustainability, eligibility for debt reduction, the amount of debt reduction needed, conditionality, and modalities regarding the provision of necessary funds, including those for the multilateral financial institutions affected. There should also be a commitment on the part of creditors to implementing fully and swift any recommendation of this panel regarding the writing-off of unpayable debt.

Limited Liability and Sovereign Governments

Mediation or arbitration in the event of effective bankruptcy is not the only or main ways in which our domestic legal systems balance the interests of economic development against those of creditors. The key instruments in law are corporate personality and limited liability of the corporation. The earliest corporations were in fact governmental bodies, especially towns. The idea of a legal personality that continued beyond the life of the individuals running its affairs arose with the church, but by analogy was applied to municipal life. The corporation was then later seen as a useful vehicle for commercial life; that is, the joint stock company.

Countries are not, of course, commercial enterprises, and citizens are not simply shareholders. But countries—deemed still to be sovereign states—are like corporations, going on beyond the life of the current office-holders, and binding their successors.

The original corporations, set up by charter, probably had limited liability (that is, their members or stockholders were liable only to a specified extent). This included few traders, who were normally liable personally to the full extent of their own, or their partnership's, debts. In England, it was not till the mid nineteenth century that the protection of limited liability was granted for most trading purposes. In 1852, a Mercantile Law Commission was set up to consider permitting limited liability. Views were sharply divided. There were those who feared, in effect, moral hazard, and an increase in the risk of fraud.

The commission was cautious, but supported limited liability for two purposes: (a) for those "many useful enterprises calculated to produce benefit to the public and profit to those who engage in them" that are "of such magnitude that no private partnership can be expected to provide the funds necessary ... of which docks, railways, and extensive shipping companies may be taken as examples, and (b) "there are others of a more limited character, from which benefit to the humbler classes of society may be expected to accrue ... such as baths and wash-houses, lodging-houses and reading rooms, to the establishment of which by large capitalists there is little inducement." (Manchester 1980)

That is, both major infrastructure and social service investment needed limited liability for the developer. Thus, the wider case for protecting developers and investors from unlimited liability for losses won out. However, sovereign states were never granted such protection. Nor is limited liability protection applied to some international operators, such as Lloyds of London, whose guarantors felt that the profits they could make outweighed any risks of loss.

The Relationship between State and Citizen

Partly as a result of legal protection and IMF financial protectionism, the international financial system operates well for corporations, shareholders, and investors, who, despite much rhetoric about markets, are protected from risk and the "wrath of market forces." Shareholders and investors have fought hard over centuries to achieve protection from the unlimited liabilities that may be incurred by the directors of companies.

There are of course, exceptions, but they are few. All over the world shareholders now enjoy the legal protection of "limited liability." Not so the citizens of indebted nations like Nigeria. This is particularly unjust in light of international commitments on human rights and because there is a social contract between every nation state and its citizens. Debtor sovereign states, like all states, are there to serve their citizens. They cannot remove, sell, or give away their fundamental human rights.

Though the state can require citizens to pay taxes, the liability is limited, to such tax payments as do not abrogate their human rights. Thus the country as a whole has a limited liability, limited to such tax payments as do not abrogate the human rights of their citizens. Clearly, these concepts still have to be worked out and agreed internationally, but we assert that it cannot be ethical, just, or fair for states to be paying out more in debt servicing than in spending on the health, clean water, sanitation, and education that are the fundamental human rights of their citizens.

States cannot hold their people responsible for the unlimited liabilities caused by foreign debts, negotiated in secret, and often corruptly. If debtor nation states could be compared to corporations, if their governments were to be seen as boards of directors, then external creditors could be put on notice that the shareholders—citizens or stakeholders—have limited liability for loans made recklessly.

However, as things stand, just like the unfortunate aristocrats of Britain who invested in Lloyds, the people of debtor nations bear unlimited responsibility for liabilities incurred by their "boards of directors": sovereign debtor governments, in collusion with foreign reditors. No wonder we encounter resistance in debtor nations like Argentina, Turkey, Pakistan, Indonesia, Zambia, and Thailand, to name but a few.

The Example of Kosovo

The Universal Declaration on Human Rights, Article 3, asserts that "everyone has the right to life, liberty, and security of person." Article 22 makes plain that "everyone as a member of society has the right to social security and is entitled to realization, through national effort and international co-operation and in accordance with the organization and resources of each state, of the economic, social, and cultural rights indispensable for his dignity and the free development of his personality." A similar set of rights is set out in the UN Charter.

NATO went to war in Kosovo in the name of humanitarian intervention. The legality of the armed intervention was challenged, but the fact that massive denials of human rights can undermine a region as well as a country is not in dispute. A British Foreign Office briefing, posted on its official website at the time of NATO's air campaign, stated: "The military action being taken against the forces of the Federal Republic of Yugoslavia is legal. It is justified as an exceptional measure to prevent an overwhelming humanitarian catastrophe. Such action is justifiable in international law in support of purposes laid down by the United Nations Security Council, even without the Council's express authorization." (Krivosheev 2001)

At the time of the first air action by NATO in Kosovo, 65,000 people were estimated to have been made homeless. This gives us some yardstick by which to judge future action or inaction for "humanitarian intervention" to defend human rights.

The United Nations estimates that 7 million children die each year because money that could be spent on health is instead diverted to foreign creditors in the form of debt repayments. (UNDP, *Human Development Report* 1997). The example of Zambia demonstrates the direct impact of debt on the life chances of millions of people infected with HIV/AIDS.

The Food and Agriculture Organization (FAO) of the United Nations has detailed the impact of the debt crisis of 1997 on the people of Indonesia. According to the FAO, the proportion of Indonesians who are undernourished almost certainly doubled from 6 percent of the population in 1995–1957 to 12 percent in 1999. And the current figure could be as high as 18 percent. Reduced consumption of foods rich in protein and micronutrients led to sharp increases in the number of wasted children and enteric mothers. The debt crisis added 10 to 20 million people to the ranks of the undernourished in Indonesia alone, just one of the five nations affected by the reckless lending decisions of foreign creditors in 1997 (FAO 1991). These numbers overshadow the 65,000 whose human rights are accepted to have been denied in Kosovo.

Humanitarian intervention to defend the human rights of a billion people in indebted nations will result in a transformation of the global economy. Intervention will challenge the dominance of finance capital. And creditors will invariably be disciplined.

Conclusion

There are many ways of disciplining finance capital: most effectively through capital controls, by extending limited liability to sovereign states, by introducing an international insolvency law that would allow states to "seek protection from their creditors," and by the introduction of a Tobin tax. However, the most urgently needed discipline is the massive cancellation of the unpayable debts of the poorest countries. Decisions about what is "unpayable" should not be decided by creditors, but by independent boards of arbitration overseen by, and held accountable to, the citizens of debtor nations.

There will be ferocious resistance to this challenge to international finance capital, in particular by the Anglo-American alliance. However, finance capital faces even greater challenges from the anarchy caused by the reckless and excessive liberalization of capital flows.

While, this anarchy currently parades as prosperity in some parts of the West, there are signs (in Japan, Turkey, Argentina, and elsewhere) that the system is sliding into a deflationary depression. Finance capital, which has not learned the lessons of the 1920s, may have to be rescued from its own irresponsibility, and before economies and societies are once again destroyed by the reckless greed that drives liberalization and deflationary policies.

Just as in Kosovo, so in debtor nations like Nigeria. There is now a clear, ethical, and economic case for humanitarian intervention to subordinate the interests of finance capital and to restore human rights to at least a billion innocent people.

References

Cornish, W. R., and G. de N. Clark. 1989. *Laws and Society in England 1750–1950*. London: Sweet and Maxwell.

FAO (Food and Agriculture Organization). 1999. *The State of Food Insecurity in the World.* Rome.
Greider, William. 1997. *One World, Ready or Not.* New York: Simon and Shuster.
Kelly, James A. 1998. "East Asia's Rolling Crises: Worries for the Year of the Tiger." Report. Center for Strategic and International Studies Pacific Forum, Pacnet 1, January 2
Krivosheev, Dennis. 2001. "NATO's Military Campaign Over Kosovo, 24 April-10 June 1999." Unpublished.
Levitt, Kari Polanyi. 1999. *The Contemporary Significance of The Great Transformation.* Location of publisher: Publisher.[Au: Pls supply]
Manchester, A. H. 1980. *A Modern Legal History of England and Wales 1750–1950.* London: Butterworths.
Raffer, Kunibert. 1992. "What's Good for the United States Must be Good for the World: Advocating an International Chapter 9 Insolvency." Paper presented to the Kreisky Forum Symposium, Vienna, September.
Raffer, Kunibert. 1999. "An International Insolvency Procedure for Sovereign States." Paper presented at the Colloquium on Legitimacy of Debt Repayment, Observatoire de la Finance, Geneva September 24–26.
Sojourners Magazine. 1998. "Jesus' New Economy of Grace: The Biblical Vision of Sabbath Economics." July-August.
Ugarteche, Oscar. 2000. "A Fair and Transparent Process: Lessons from the Southern States of the U.S. Between 1841 and 1930, the Inter-Allied Debts 1919–1931, the German Debts 1924–1953." Unpublished.

Index

A
Abdulsalami Abubakar regime 171
Abuja v-vi, 3, 112, 114, 148, 199, 212-213, 222, 257-258
Africa iii, viii, 1-2, 19, 23-26, 28-29, 34-35, 41, 48, 51-60, 65-66, 70-73, 75-85, 87, 89, 91-92, 96-98, 101, 104-107, 120, 144, 146-150, 155, 165, 174, 212-213, 222, 234, 254, 257
Africa Growth and Opportunity Act (AGOA) viii, 51
African Development Bank (AfDB) vi, viii, 75, 83, 85-89, 100, 173
African Development Fund (ADF) 87, 89
African economies 53
African Institute for Applied Economics 3
Ajayi, Ibi 105

C
Callisto Madavo iii, 91
capital flight iii, 11, 13, 28, 49, 53-54, 76, 105-107, 109, 111, 113, 115, 117, 119, 121, 123, 125, 127-141, 143, 145, 147-149, 151, 226, 228, 233-234, 262

Central Bank of Nigeria (CBN) viii, 2, 16, 148, 173-175, 179-180, 182, 184, 196-198, 208-209, 212-213
Chhibber, Ajay 35, 70
Collier, Paul iv, 225
Commonwealth of Independent States 25
Comprehensive Development Framework viii, 33
Crown Agents Consultants 180

D
debt cancellation iv, 13-14, 37, 67, 92, 99-100, 147, 203, 217-224, 237, 239-240, 243, 245, 262-263
Debt Management Office (DMO) v, viii, 3, 5-7, 18, 41, 65, 112, 114, 161-162, 169, 179-184, 193, 209-210, 252-253
Debt Recording and Management System viii, 174, 210
Debt Relief International 237, 242, 253
debt rescheduling 32, 34, 125, 135
debt-overhang theory 134
debt-service ratio 197, 201
Department for International Development vi, 3, 179,

277

228
domestic debt 2, 16, 42, 76-77, 179, 182, 184
Dutch disease 231

E
Enweze, Cyril iii, 2, 75
Extended Structural Adjustment Facility (ESAF) viii, 33, 61
external debt iii, 2, 4, 6-8, 14, 16, 34, 65, 75-76, 81, 83, 105-107, 109-125, 127, 129, 131-139, 141-150, 168-172, 175, 179, 195, 197-198, 200-202, 204-205, 207-209, 212-213, 254, 266

F
Foreign Operations Department 175, 180

G
G7 240, 2-246, 252, 266
GDP (Gross Domestic Product) viii, 2, 9, 11, 25, 32, 36, 43, 49, 55, 59, 63, 65, 67, 70, 76, 84, 93, 96-97, 116, 136, 138-139, 141, 166, 201-202, 230-232, 238, 242, 244, 261-262
General Abacha 231, 262
globalization 51-53, 56, 64, 70-71, 143

governance iv, 1, 27, 52, 58, 66, 69, 73, 76-77, 80-81, 85, 89, 95, 98, 146, 153, 156, 167, 169, 171, 173, 175-179, 181, 183, 185, 187, 189, 191, 193, 195, 198, 204
Gross National Product (GNP) viii, 26, 84, 96, 101, 116-120, 122, 131-132, 218-219

H
Highly Indebted Poor Countries Initiative (HIPC) viii, 4, 14, 40, 60-62, 73, 76, 83, 86-87, 92-96, 98-99, 102, 146, 218-224, 227, 238-243, 245-248, 251, 254, 260-261, 269
HIV/AIDS epidemic 10, 26-27, 43, 55, 78, 82, 84, 93, 97, 183, 217, 222, 224, 263, 274

I
Incremental Capital Output Ratio (IOCR) 28
Institutional Investor Risk Rating (IIRR) viii, 233
International Bank for Reconstruction and Development (IBRD) viii, 61, 95, 100-101,

212, 239, 244, 248, 260-261
International Development Association (IDA) viii, 47, 61, 95, 100-101, 239-241, 244-247, 250, 252, 260-261
International Monetary and Financial Committee (IMFC) viii, 155-156
International Monetary Fund (IMF) vi, viii, 6, 32, 61, 73, 88, 92, 108, 124-126, 131, 145, 148-151, 156, 171, 181, 206, 220, 238, 240, 243-245, 247-248, 252, 256-258, 260-261, 266, 268, 271

J

Jubilee 2000 64, 227, 255, 257, 261, 263-264, 269

L

Least developed Countries (LDCs) 26, 44, 51, 58, 84
London Club of Commercial Creditors 170

M

Martín, Matthew iv, 237
Millennium Development Goals (MDGs) 9, 263
Ministry of Finance 12, 108, 158-161, 172-173, 175, 179, 196, 199, 208-209
Ministry of National Planning 208-209

N

National Assembly 18, 223, 259
NATO 273, 276
Nigerian Telecommunications (NITEL) 223
North American Free Trade Association 54

O

Obadan, Mike iv, 5, 12-13, 195, 213
Obasanjo, Olusegun v, 3, 5, 11, 42, 145, 172, 178, 217, 257
Okonjo-Iweala, Ngozi i, iii-iv, 1, 12-13, 167
Organization for Economic Cooperation and Development (OECD) viii, 63, 70, 84, 96-98, 101, 157, 159-160, 162, 177, 256, 260, 266
Overseas Development Assistance (ODA) viii, 28, 32, 41, 50, 54-55, 59-63, 84

P

parastatals 2, 176, 209, 248
Paris Club 5-7, 14, 34, 37, 61, 103-104, 112, 170-

173, 177, 180-181, 183, 195-196, 203, 206, 210-211, 243-247, 252, 254, 258-259, 266
Poland 14, 73, 165
poverty iii, viii, 1, 9-10, 15, 19, 21, 23-27, 29-33, 35, 37-43, 45, 47, 49, 51-59, 61-69, 71-73, 77, 79-81, 84-86, 89, 94, 97-98, 104, 145, 218, 222-223, 227-229, 234-235, 237, 239-240, 245, 247-248, 250-253, 255-256, 258-260
privatization 10, 16-17, 49-50, 206, 223

R

Regional Member Countries (RMC) viii, 83, 89
Republic of Congo 96

S

Sachs, Jeffrey iv, 5, 9, 13, 54, 63, 68-69, 71, 217, 267-268
Sao Tome and Principe 125
Sierra Leone 96
Soludo, Charles i, iii, 1-2, 5, 23, 33, 54, 63, 70-71
Somalia 96
Sudan 96, 125

U

Uganda 15, 26, 55, 99, 231-233
UN Charter 273
UNDP (United Nations Development Program) vi, 25, 27, 58, 71, 274

W

Wealth of Nations—Adam Smith 264-266
welfare state 52, 56
Wheeler, Graeme iv, 13, 155
World Bank vi, viii, 6, 24, 29, 33, 35, 38, 40, 44, 51, 55, 58-59, 61, 66-68, 70-71, 88, 91-92, 95, 108-109, 111, 113, 117, 131, 145, 147-149, 151-152, 155-156, 167, 169, 175, 184, 206, 212, 219, 225, 228-230, 234, 239, 244, 247, 252, 260-261, 266, 268
World Social and Sustainable Development Summit (WSSD) viii, 59

Z

Zaire 37, 125
Zambia 44, 125, 272, 274